TELLING

A Latin@ Anthology on Language Experience

Edited by
Louis G. Mendoza & Toni Nelson Herrera

TELLING TONGUES
A Latin@ Anthology on Language Experience

Edited

by

Louis G. Mendoza

&

Toni Nelson Herrera

Calaca Press
National City, Califas

Red Salmon Press
Austin, Tejas

2007

First printing published by Calaca Press and Red Salmon Press in 2007.

ISBN 0-9717035-8-2

Cover art by Nuvia Crisol Guerra.
Cover/interior design and layout by Cal A. Vera.
Illustrations on pages 143-144 © 2002 Cecilia Isabel Méndez.

The following appeared elsewhere:
Spanish at School Translates to Suspension © 2005, *The Washington Post*. Lengualistic Algo: Spoken-Broken Word, *When Skin Peels* (Calaca Press, 1999). Mother Tongue: Unman Chant, *Roll Call* (Third World Press). The Latina in Me, *Waking Up American* (Seal Press). Buggarones, *Furia* (Milkweed Editions, 2005). Commercial Break, *Pepper Spray (*Momotombo Press).

Acknowledgements
Muchas gracias to the research assistants who assisted in the process of gathering materials and communicating with our contributors. At the University of Texas at San Antonio, Patricia Trujillo (ABD in Latino Literary and Cultural Studies in the Department of English) was instrumental in the early stages. At the University of Minnesota, Brittany Clausell provided important support work in bringing this project to fruition. This project received subvention funds from the College of Liberal Arts at the University of Minnesota.

Calaca Press
P.O. Box 2309
National City, Califas 91951
(619) 434-9036
calacapress@cox.net
www.calacapress.com
www.myspace.com/calacalandia

Calaca Press is a Chicano family-owned small publishing house dedicated to publishing and producing unknown, emerging, and established progressive Chican@ and Latin@ voices.

Red Salmon Press
1801-A S. First St.
Austin, Tejas 78704
(512) 416-8885
revolu@swbell.net

Red Salmon Arts is dedicated to the development of emerging writers, the promotion of indigenous, Chicana/o, Latina/o literature, providing outlets and mechanisms for cultural exchange and sharing the retrieval of a people's history with a commitment to social justice.

Hecho en Aztlán.

c/s

Spanish At School Translates to Suspension

By T.R. Reid - Washington Post Staff Writer
Friday, December 9, 2005; A03

KANSAS CITY, Kan., Dec. 8 -- Most of the time, 16-year-old Zach Rubio converses in clear, unaccented American teen-speak, a form of English in which the three most common words are "like," "whatever" and "totally." But Zach is also fluent in his dad's native language, Spanish -- and that's what got him suspended from school.

"It was, like, totally not in the classroom," the high school junior said, recalling the infraction. "We were in the, like, hall or whatever, on restroom break. This kid I know, he's like, 'Me prestas un dolar?' ['Will you lend me a dollar?'] Well, he asked in Spanish; it just seemed natural to answer that way. So I'm like, 'No problema.'"

But that conversation turned out to be a big problem for the staff at the Endeavor Alternative School, a small public high school in an ethnically mixed blue-collar neighborhood. A teacher who overheard the two boys sent Zach to the office, where Principal Jennifer Watts ordered him to call his father and leave the school.

Watts, whom students describe as a disciplinarian, said she can't discuss the case. But in a written "discipline referral" explaining her decision to suspend Zach for 1 1/2 days, she noted: "This is not the first time we have [asked] Zach and others to not speak Spanish at school."

Since then, the suspension of Zach Rubio has become the talk of the town in both English and Spanish newspapers and radio shows. The school district has officially rescinded his punishment and said that speaking a foreign language is not grounds for suspension. Meanwhile, the Rubio family has retained a lawyer, who says a civil rights lawsuit may be in the offing.

The tension here surrounding that brief exchange in a high school hall reflects a broader national debate over the language Americans should speak amid a wave of Hispanic immigration.

The National Council of La Raza, a Hispanic advocacy group, says that 20 percent of the U.S. school-age population is Latino. For half of those Latino students, the native language is Spanish.

Conflicts are bursting out nationwide over bilingual education, "English-only" laws, Spanish-language publications and advertising, and other linguistic collisions. Language concerns have been a key aspect of the growing political movement to reduce immigration.

"There's a lot of backlash against the increasing Hispanic population," said D.C. school board member Victor A. Reinoso. "We've seen some of it in the D.C. schools. You see it in some cities, where people complain that their tax money shouldn't be used to print public notices in Spanish. And there have been cases where schools want to ban foreign languages."

Some advocates of an English-only policy in U.S. schools say that it is particularly important for students from immigrant families to use the nation's dominant language.

California Gov. Arnold Schwarzenegger (R) made that point this summer when he vetoed a bill authorizing various academic subjects to be tested in Spanish in the state's public schools. "As an immigrant," the Austrian-born governor said, "I know the importance of mastering English as quickly and as comprehensively as possible."

Hispanic groups generally agree with that, but they emphasize the value of a multilingual citizenry. "A fully bilingual young man like Zach Rubio should be considered an asset to the community," said Janet Murguia, national president of La Raza.

The influx of immigrants has reached every corner of the country -- even here in Kansas City, which is about as far as a U.S. town can be from a border. Along Southwest Boulevard, a main street through some of the older neighborhoods, there are blocks where almost every shop and restaurant has signs written in Spanish.

"Most people, they don't care where you're from," said Zach's father, Lorenzo Rubio, a native of Veracruz, Mexico, who has lived in Kansas City for a quarter-century. "But sometimes, when they hear my accent, I get this, sort of, 'Why don't you go back home?'"

Rubio, a U.S. citizen, credits U.S. immigration law for his decision to fight his son's suspension.

"You can't just walk in and become a citizen," he said. "They make you take this government test. I studied for that test, and I learned that in America, they can't punish you unless you violate a written policy."

Rubio said he remembered that lesson on Nov. 28, when he received a call from Endeavor Alternative saying his son had been suspended.

"So I went to the principal and said, 'My son, he's not suspended for fighting, right? He's not suspended for disrespecting anyone. He's suspended for speaking Spanish in the hall?' So I asked her to show me the written policy about that. But they didn't have one.

Rubio then called the superintendent of the Turner Unified School District, which operates the school. The district immediately rescinded Zach's suspension, local media reported. The superintendent did not respond to several requests to comment for this article.

Since then, the issue of speaking Spanish in the hall has not been raised at the school, Zach said. "I know it would be, like, disruptive if I answered in Spanish in the classroom. I totally don't do that. But outside of class now, the teachers are like, 'Whatever.'"

For Zach's father, and for the Hispanic organizations that have expressed concern, the suspension is not a closed case. "Obviously they've violated his civil rights," said Chuck Chionuma, a lawyer in Kansas City, Mo., who is representing the Rubio family. "We're studying what form of legal redress will correct the situation."

Said Rubio: "I'm mainly doing this for other Mexican families, where the legal status is kind of shaky and they are afraid to speak up. Punished for speaking Spanish? Somebody has to stand up and say: This is wrong."

TABLE OF CONTENTS

LANGUAGE PRACTICE AND CULTURAL LOYALTY: IDENTITY AND BELONGING AMONG LATIN@S IN THE U.S.

[I]f you really want to hurt me, talk badly about my language. Ethnic identity is twin skin to linguistic identity—I am my language. Until I can take pride in my language, I cannot take pride in myself.

– Gloria Anzaldúa

So proclaims the late Gloria Anzaldúa, one of the most significant and articulate cultural critics of our time who asked us to speak the unspoken and in so doing to voice the sources of our collective and individual strengths and weaknesses. For vast numbers of Chicanas and Chicanos, and many, many others, Anzaldúa's work was a liberating force that spoke forcefully and bluntly about institutional violence, inter-cultural aggression, and intra-cultural contradictions without regard for academic niceties or piety. As co-editors of this anthology on language experiences, both of us feel a debt of gratitude for her courage. In presenting a variety of perspectives on this topic, our goal with this anthology is to open a dialogue on this matter that will acknowledge the complexities undergirding people's language experiences in a manner that pushes the boundaries of discussions about Latina/o language practices in a different direction than Anzaldúa did. In our discussions about the need for an anthology that challenged the persistent link between language practice and cultural identity, particularly assertions that went a step further and suggested that language and cultural loyalty were synonymous and necessarily co-existent, Anzaldúa's assertion, quoted above, that ethnicity and linguistic identity were one and the same served as a touchstone for our conflicted relationship to language politics. This was not, of course, because we fail to understand the politics of language rights and the violence associated with forcing people to speak the dominant language, nor because we think the everyday language we speak doesn't matter. We know it does. What we knew in our hearts, and we believe we are not alone in this, is that the complexities of our history as Mexicans in the United States were such that one could not, indeed should not, assert absolutes about language practice and cultural loyalty without vigilant regard for social context that influences and shapes available choices. Rather than view the relationship between language practice and cultural loyalty as having a one-to-one correspondence, we argue that these points of reference for identity exist on a continuum of experience, one that is capable of shifting over time and is contingent on choice, opportunity, community, and a myriad of other factors. Stated another way, our observations tell us that people's relationships with language is dynamic, fluid, and circumstantial.

Lest we be misunderstood, it is important to say that we understand, appreciate, and value language facility, retention and acquisition. While one might be able to argue that language is a significant element of one's nationality, we assert that it is imperative for ethnic minorities, even the majority-minority, to be mindful of the complex and vexed relationship between nationality and ethnic nationalism. Creative writer and scholar, Gustavo Pérez Firmat asserts that,

> For most of us…the language we speak is a fundamental component of our nationality, and hence our sense of who we are. That is why, when we want to question someone's claims about his nationality, we often take aim at his language habits: "Funny, you don't sound like an American." … The complexity of these feelings [about language practices] suggests that the notion of language loyalty, useful as it is, does not do justice to an individual's attachment to his or her languages. (1-2)

Nor, we would add, to one's cultural affiliation.

Speaking as individuals who advocate on behalf of the Chicano community in our scholarship and community-based work, we have also each been confronted many times over with challenges to our lack of Spanish language proficiency and the oft unstated implication that this casts our cultural integrity under suspicion. Indeed, one way we learned to respond to this is to become a master storyteller in reminding people about the relationship between the history of colonialism and the systematic delegitimization of one's native tongue. Then, too, many proud nationalists need to be reminded that Spanish, too, is a colonizer's language. From both an ethno-nationalist to an official nationalist point of view, language usage is often seen as a measure of assimilation. For many U.S. Latinos, retaining Spanish as a dominant language and or being bilingual is seen as a signifier of cultural loyalty and as an asset. We must keep in mind though that many recent arrivals know, recognize, and value the acquisition of English and are willing to pay the price of language loss to enter into the economic mainstream. We are not saying it is a price worth paying, but merely pointing out this fact.

On the other hand, despite evidence pointing to persistent linguistic assimilation by new immigrants, U.S. nativists continue to argue that those who speak and retain their native tongue, particularly if that native tongue is other than English, represent a threat to the social fabric of the U.S. One need only acknowledge the ongoing efforts to pass legislation making English the official language of the United States (globalization be damned!) to see how language practice is a battleground for immigration issues and civil rights. It appears that nativists are willing to tolerate language retention by non-English speakers only if it is accompanied by the price of political, social, and economic exclusion. Clearly, language practice is fodder for public debate on claims to national authenticity and cultural citizenship.

The inspiration for this project emerges from the recognition that it is a critically important time in our history to articulate the complexity of being Latina/o in the U.S. and to understand the implications this has for navigating the many issues surrounding language usage that this involves. By gathering an array of voices engaging with, but in no way able to entirely represent, the theme of "language experience" and looking at how those experiences shape the lives of Latina/os it is hoped that a sense of the complexity of this lived reality will become apparent. The goal is to express the range of those experiences from a variety of vantage points and to enable these voices to express how language informs reality and is manifested in the everyday lives of Latina/os.

This collection emerges from the basic idea that no one story could represent the lived complexities of what it means to be Latina/o and what it is like to have, to lose, or to gain the ability to speak Spanish over the course of one's life, much less the lives of all the members of one's family or larger community. If one were to trace a historical trajectory for language usage for Chicano/as in the United States for example, the story would shift and turn based on region and time period, and on waves of immigration and deportation. One generation of a family may have lived through segregated schooling in the thirties in South Texas, while also having gained from the relative opportunity to learn English or Spanish by traveling in the Midwest as part of the migrant stream. One family member may have been adept at multiple languages and another more monolingual in practice. Like the colors of our skin, our lived realities are shaded and distinct, and not clear indicators of any one thing. That is why we have gathered these voices together—to provide a space for dialogue that may move past the page and into classrooms and homes, political meetings and working settings, in the bedroom and over the phone between lovers and friends,between siblings that went to college and those that did not, amongst parents who do and don't want their children to learn Spanish, and children who want or don't want to learn it too.

This project emerges out of many strands of experience. We believed that creating a space to tell these stories together was more powerful than just telling our own stories or those of our friends and family members experiences with language. We wanted to go deeper and create a space for a larger dialogue that would show the complexity and contradictions of Latina/o language experiences as an act of building political solidarity, and out of a desire not to be silent. We wanted it to be a space that could help heal the wounds of the collective damage that has been inflicted upon the generations who had the Spanish beaten out of them and who subsequently made the difficult choice not to transfer those skills to their children, only to have the world shift so much that only a few decades later they were being told that if only they were bi-lingual they could get better jobs. We wanted a political space, written onto paper, that said it was okay to be at whatever stage of knowing or not knowing Spanish and still claim Latina/o identity and culture. We wanted to avoid the dualism of "bi-lingualism", and create instead a map of experience that had many signposts and routes leading in different directions, instead of a linear model with a straight line pointing left to right from "pure culture" to "assimilation."

Before the submissions came we had a hunch, from our lived experiences, that the story of Latina/o language experiences was much more complex than had been told. Other anthologies have addressed issues of language usage, but these have drawn mainly on scholarly voices or the writings of popular authors or the singular perspective of one person. This collection instead, brings together the fresh voices of more experienced writers with those just starting out, and in a range of styles from poetry to memoir, and from prose essay to fiction. The layering of these voices—their shared understandings and differences in practices, together make up the composite picture we hoped this project would create.

As became clear in the aftermath of the 2000 census, Latinos have emerged as the nation's largest minority due to a steady flow of legal and extra-legal immigration as well as the cumulative impact of higher birthrates in the last few decades. As the implications of these demographic shifts are still being explored for their impact on public policy, electoral politics, the economy, and public discourse, it is clear that this Latinoization of the U.S. cannot be ignored or dismissed. Latinas/os are often presented in media, academic, and popular discourse in a traditional immigrant model that measures assimilation solely through language usage. As we argue above, we find this model to be insufficient for capturing the complexity of lived experience. Though we find the data gathered by social science research, such as the 2004 study on Latino language usage and acculturation by the Pew Center, to be insightful, we believe it can also flatten out the nuances of that experience. It is our hope that by presenting a wide array of original writings in multiple genres the texture and depth of lived experience will emerge and that we can gain insight into how Latina/o self-identification is inflected through a variety of language experiences. Equally important is the opportunity a collection like this provides for people to represent themselves in ways that are excluded by academic and political discourse. Even public policy debates do not allow for people to articulate the role of language in their lives, particularly the profound way that deep sentiments, spirituality, and a sense of self is informed by the way one speaks and how those articulations are perceived, received, or simply not heard by others.

The rich diversity of the collection here mirrors not only the complexity of the people who self-identify as Latina/o, but shows how language experience can be a prism through which almost any aspect of life can be viewed. The collection includes childhood stories on the role of language in identity formation, interactions between lovers, workplace relations or between family members, educational or religious experiences, interactions among Latinas/os, and with other cultural groups. We believe that the diversity of perspectives, voices, languages, and styles included here provides insight into the fluid dynamic of social, class, cultural, communal, and national identity formation and provide insight into how identity is formed, lost, maintained, or otherwise negotiated through language usage.

Because we wanted to respect the wide array of themes the authors presented here address in their contributions to the collection, we have chose not to organize the work thematically for fear that we would reduce the authors' primary meaning to fit into a rubric of our design. In light of this we opted to organize the work by genre, even as we acknowledge and value the experimental approaches some of these authors practice in their poetry, fiction, and testimonios. The range of themes that the authors touch upon are numerous and show the incredible subtlety and impact of struggles with the issues raised by language usage. From intra-ethnic tensions or grappling with the hostility of the dominant social order in a variety of ways, to one's private internal struggles, and the moments that those struggles spill out into relationships with friends and family, issues of language shape and are informed by experience.

Many selections reveal a sense that language and the ability to define oneself are crucial and critical ongoing practices. Whether a part of multi-ethnic families or communities, the authors highlight feelings of rejection, disappointment, joy and triumph in their efforts to make sense of the world and their place in it. We see also the importance of memory here, how the pain of previous generations gets carried around in one's psyche, and mingles with present difficulties—existing like open wounds that any amount of limón y sal can painfully augment. There is a also a keen sense of awareness by these authors of being in a particular historic moment, and being part of a movement with political purpose that is gaining momentum as many authors actively resist the oppressions they feel on many levels by seeking to make language expressions more public. Some of the pieces engage the current "Spanglish buzz" and media hype surrounding Latina/os with incisive humor and challenge the self-appointed or selected standard bearers who would speak for them. As one author puts it, "It is just no longer as simple as you are either assimilated or newly immigrated."

There are echoes between the writings—that ever recurring moment when you will be asked about your language ability in line or at odds with, in the inquisitor's mind, your phenotypical and cultural attributes—and you'll think about how you have responded before, and how you'll respond the next time it happens. The writers here also touch on issues of ethnic "authenticity" and challenge simplistic notions of what it means to be Latina/o. We also see how language usage is reflective of debates over the politics of inclusion and exclusion and community identification. Education is also an important recurring theme beginning in elementary and going all the way through higher education, from the indignities of the classroom, to deep feelings of rejection, to harnessing the power of the written word to fight back. The injuries of class and how those often intersect with language also becomes clear.

Language also exists here on a spiritual level, a few of the pieces are offered up as prayers for protection from the abuses and mistreatment in which language plays a part. Many authors touch on issues of how language has been shaped by our attitudes and experiences about gender, sexuality, and sexual identity and thus we get a sense of how language is also found in unspoken looks and in touch. Others talk about how language choices, limitations, and capacities affirm as well as frustrate our relationships with others in a constantly unfolding drama. These authors speak to questions of how language has been used as a basis for both division and exclusion amongst Latina/os themselves while at the same time dealing with the mainstream's perception of linguistic practices and the homogenization of U.S. Latina/os by the popular media.

We are also proud to note the extraordinary creativity and array of artistic approaches that all of the authors bring to the discussion. We are deeply impressed by their abilities to express these struggles over language in some many thoughtful and compelling ways. From plays, to interviews, to powerful essays, from the imagined to the real, these authors pushed the boundaries, exceeded expectations, and offer up their work as a source of inspiration for all. One particularly unique submission was a series of drawings along with an artist's statement exploring the metaphor of kitchen tools as a way of understanding the slicing, dicing and mixing of language practices. Another reads like a commercial for "what a Mexican can bring to your poetry." Yet another selection transports you back in time to Vietnam when the Chicano author discovered his own humanity during war by connecting with a Vietnamese child via language. Overall, language is shown as something that helps people to connect and transcend limitations which we believe has huge political implications.

The multiplicity of perspectives offered here demonstrate the complexity and rich diversity of U.S. Latina/os. The decision to include as wide array of people with different national histories, including Spain, was made to embrace this complexity rather than opt to present a more cohesive picture of latinidad. As is evident the authors represent a broad contrast of lived experiences, but also have shared realities. What we have compiled is a portrayal of the wide range of experiences that reflects the complexity of Latina/o language experiences and which, taken collectively, asserts meaning about the significance of language as a means of self-fashioning and self-identification. The ability to define oneself and represent one's experience, as part of a larger collective dialogue is an important political act. We do not believe there is a singular or reductive way to capture this experience, but hope to promote dialogue amongst groups and challenge mainstream America's conception about the meaning of Latina/o language practices and what it says about how they see themselves and their place in society and the world.

POETRY

Olga A. García Echeverría

LENGUALISTIC ALGO: SPOKEN-BROKEN WORD

¿Qué quieren conmigo los puristas?
all tongue tied
and sitting proper
behind fat stoic dictionaries

I've already eaten the thin white skeletons
of foreign words
choked on the bones of inglés only
learned the art of speaking in codes
and code switching
learned to spit palabras
out of boca abierta
bullets
fire
fuego
poems

have already been witness to silence
to white-haired first grade teacher
bringing finger to lips and saying
Shhhhh! Speak English
You're in America now
Speak English

Mi bisabuela fue yaqui
mi abuela mexicana
mi madre mestiza
¿Y yo?

Your worst linguistic nightmare
hecho realidad

Aquí se le echa de todo
East Los Attitude
Chile chipotle
Chicana power fist held in air

Aquí el inglés se quita sus moños
wears pantalones huangos
and dances slow motion to oldies

Aquí el inglés trips over itself
y el español comes down
off its high horse
cruises down Whittier Boulevard
in a beat-up station wagon
in a minivan
in a cherry-red impala lowrider
wátchala it rides the bus
eats chile spiced mangos
and elotes smothered in mayonesa
it learns to say pa' instead of para
'ca instead of acá
'lla instead of allá
travel pa' 'ca y pa' 'lla
pa' 'lla y pa' 'ca
pa' Caló
¡Órale!

Somos las chicas patas lenguas que no se rajan
cruzando linguistic fronteras sin papeles
illegal tongues jumping over barbed wire fences
running como las cucarachas
¡Córrele cuquita! ¡Córrele!

Aquí el lenguaje existe en el momento
que Conejo hits up Pablo for a ride
Come on vato give me
un aventón to the marqueta
y Pablo lo manda a la fregada
with a wave of a hand y con
¡Chale dude! ¿Qué me ves? ¿cara de taxi cab?

Aquí se usa lo que sirve
el rascuache
el mestizaje
las leftovers
y lo yet-to-be born

Aquí cada palabra está viva—respira
and all the spoken-broken words
the Wátchalas
los Éses and Ésas of the world
stand up in defiance and shout

Hey! Ain't I a Word?
caigo from the hungry mouths of thousands
salgo como bala en los barrios de Califas
broto como lluvia en el desierto de Arizona
canto mi Tex-Mex junto a Flaco Jiménez
and tell me, Ain't I a Word?

Los académicos me ignoran
los puristas dicen que contamino
Webster y el Pequeño Larousse no me conocen
y Random House me escupe
¡No manchen!

Aquí mi lenguaje no se detiene
cada nueva palabra remembers
relives speaks the many conquests
of our bleeding tongues

Our language
como cuerpo de serpiente
moves
shape shifts
sheds
en un instante muere
y aún vuelve a nacer

Margarita Engle

TRANSLATION

The printed label on the plastic package says
Ensalada Mixta
Mixed Salad

but a confident sign
on the produce department shelf
announces:

Bilingual Garden Salad

quickly leading me down pathways of thought
toward talking lettuce
and the incessant bickering
of radishes and carrots

colorful characters
from the seedy underworld
of word roots.

Rane Ramón Arroyo

MY YEARS AS A VERB

on surviving graduate school

We'd circle the Cathedral of Learning
with Glenn memorizing Spanish verbs:
cantar, to sing. Not to recant. Never

in my imagination did I ever imagine
a lover wanting to learn my language.
I'd read his index card hints and we'd

forget we were in big-boned Pittsburgh with
Andrew Carnegie's disdain of the working
class taking the shape of statues around us.

Nadar, to swim. Not to be mistaken
for nada, nothing. He once turned to me
and said, "how did you do it? learned

English until now it has to learn you?"
Most questions from lovers are rhetorical,
and when they're not, I become speechless.

*

for Julie Parson-Nesbitt,
for starting that protest petition

How I'd tire of el pobrecito,
Richard Rodriguez, always

cut up in theory classes as if
a permanent autopsy never

quite finished. I read the dolor
of praxis, of charity's thugs

collecting debts, of a brown man
with the talent of infuriating

my classmates by being
complicated, not a done deal.

Then, someone wrote on my class'
blackboard, *you think you are such*

a nigger superstar. Campus police
were sure it was a graduate student,

one required to read *The Hunger of
Memory* and starving for blood.

I thought of you, Ricardo, of your bravery
when even your own can't imagine

you dancing with a potential lover,
feeding yourself for a change.

No charges were ever brought and
I learned again that I was the crime.

*

Holiday was the closest
gay bar to campus and
also the darkest. Once,
I danced with the bar

owner's mother in the back
patio lit with red lights that
brought me back to a time
when I was part of

family fiestas. A stranger
said, with good intentions,
we're you in that porno
flick, *Aztec Ass*? I left

the bar, listened to the trees
speaking wind. The walk
home was full of echoes.
Listening does require talent.

*

I was rejected for
the fiction workshop.
Only a few of us
had to audition.
The professor said,
about my published
work, I can't comment
on this, this is foreign
to me, I can't help you.
He was right and wrong.

*

Tocar la guitarra.
Not play it,
but to touch it.
Never let it know
there are hock shops.

This dream is why I wrote
an anti-dissertation
on the Chicago Renaissance
as a model for Latino
Literature, the loss

of politics for acceptance.
I had ghosts for mirrors.
Ah, mis amigos said,
like Lorca's gypsy guitars.
No, he is not all poets.

*

Speak dirty to me in Spanish,
he said, another stranger
I brought home to windowshop

differences. Abrir, decir, pedir.
It spurred him to strip, to listen
to my heart. What are you saying?

Verbs. Olvidar, tener, sentir.
The Latin Lover has a monopoly
on the American imagination.

Anything to keep me away from
school, from the education
meant for puppeteers' first puppets.

Hungover, I'd shower and think of
classmates with envy. They were
arguing with the idea of postcolonialism,

while I straightened my bed in which,
just hours ago, I demanded a ghost to tell me
his story, Dante without a publisher.

*

At national conferences, I'd watch
brown scholars lean forward
to read my name tag: ah, Latino,
no power. ¿que tal? Ah, pues, adios.

Then there were the others, fellow
poets addicted to laughter, that manna
for the masses. I'd return to Pittsburgh
and a lover with flash cards full of

the music of my first language. We're
no one, what a luxury! Happiness
is a simple soul who is a seductive
guest (Italian films are right about this).

I now speak English, Academe, Sacrifice.
Glenn threw a party and we played
West Side Story as a postmodern wink,
a prayer for those who didn't survive English.

Rudy Garcia

SELF CONCEPT

What is it about me GOD?
Why must I always feel this odd?
I'm just a normal teenage boy
And its' not my fault en donde estoy

My parents brought me here for school
But chicanos call me a mojo fool
I go to hide way deep inside me
But there a "pinche wetback" is what I see

It seems as if I'm real contagious
Because the way I'm avoided is so outrageous
The principal really didn't welcome me
She said I'm a drop-out statistic waiting to be

A negative number towards the school's "exemplary status"
She said my presence here will eventually hurt "us"
It's never my intent to harm anyone
I simply want to study and be a good son

But why do these chicanos hurt me so?
They continuously say "back to Mexico" I should go
If they only knew how I miss my Tierra
Because there at least no soy un cualquiera

They laugh at me when ever I spic
They gawk at me like a carnys' side show freak
And the way I dress is not in style
I'm always judged, I'm always on trial

My days at school are really torture
I feel as I'm an academic poacher
Please help me dear God to understand
The ways and customs of this new land

Return my pride, my self-esteem
And to my principal I shall redeem

My use of her books, her desks, her food
And prove to her how she misunderstood

That I'm just another normal boy
And aqui me quedo y no me voy
What's really sad and odd to see
Is that my principal sure looks a lot like me.

Joe Sainz

THE FIRST DAY OF SCHOOL

The First Day of School:
Confusion, yelling, running.
Cars stop; kids jump out.
I walk slowly;
The sidewalk is my only friend.

The First Day of School:
All the beautiful book bags; } poverty)
All the beautiful thermoses;
I hug my bare notebooks,
I hug my paper bag.

The First Day of School: } language Barrier
I walk in the hallway;
I pass a sign that says: "Restrooms";
I don't understand what that means.

I walk into a room full of nine-year-old strangers;
The teacher comes near.
She welcomes me and motions me to sit;
I don't understand what she says.

She touches the seat next to one of the strangers;
He speaks my language;
I smile for the first time.
The teacher starts the lesson;
I don't understand.
She pulls down a world map;
I see a familiar land mass.

The First Day of School:
I hear meaningless words around me;
I see a hand go up.
I wish I could do that now;
Being an "A" student, I often did that in my country.
There is no "A" in my country, but there is an "Excelente."
My parents believe I am better off here;

I don't know why.

Time for recess;
I stay in my seat, not knowing.
The stranger beside me elbows me;
I get up, excitedly.
I can play; there is no language in play.
I can play; I've done that before.

I go out to the field;
The strangers line up, ball in the middle;
The strangers know what to do.
I stare from the sidelines;
I see a strange ball... a very strange ball;
I don't know what "huddle" means.

The First Day of School:
I see eyes; I hear laughter;
Why are they laughing?
I try to play;
But, I return to the sidelines.

It's lunch time;
I go, excitedly.
I can eat; there is no language in eating.
I can eat; I've done that before.
I follow the strangers to the "caf."
What is the "caf"?
I wait in line;
I watch; I follow.

The lady asks me something.
I stare; I look around;
I've lost my bilingual stranger;
She chooses my lunch at random.
I pay, but is it enough?
Is it too much?
I go. Go where?
Where do I sit?
I see my bilingual friend;
I smile.

I sit with many strangers;
"Jack"; "Jill"; "George"; "Jenny."
I hear these names for the first time.
I smile politely; I do not know at what.
My friend forgets to translate;
I smile politely; I smile politely;
I hear a bell;
What does it mean?

I follow the strangers;
I am back in class.
What a beautiful girl sitting toward the front;
I look at her and smile;
She turns away quickly.
I talk to my bilingual friend;
I ask him how to say this, and how to say that.

It's music time;
I can do music.
I open the music book, excitedly.
I can hum; there is no language in humming.
I can hum; I've done that before.
The music is stranger than the words;
I open my mouth and pretend.

The First Day of School:
I hear the loudspeaker;
I hear words; I see reactions;
I wish I had reactions.
I hear a bell; I see the clock.
The strangers pack up and dart out the door.
My friend is gone, just like my confidence.

I wave to the teacher; she waves back.
She points to the word: "Homework" on the chalkboard;
She gives me a sympathetic smile.
I smile politely, I don't know at what.
I smile politely, I smile politely.
I must ask my friend what this means;
But, he's gone... He's gone.

I exit into the bright sunshine;
I recognize sunshine.
I walk home;
I see groups of strangers walking home, laughing;
Are they laughing at me?
I walk fast.
I get home from The First Day of School...
I think about tomorrow,
and I tremble.

Steve Werkmeister

BEATING

I. Sooner

In the early seventies,
maybe I was 7, maybe I was 8,
treading my way home
through the easy promise of late spring air.
A boy I did not know—older, bigger,
white—sidled his bike up next to me,
slid off the banana seat, shoved me
with a grunt, pinned me
in the dirt. Pinwheeling through the air,
small white fists against the big
blue sky, the occasional flicks of blood.
                                The beating
didn't take much. Tears and blood and snot
slipped easily down my face, soaking into
the hand-me-down shirt and springtime grass
recently clipped.

This is why I laugh about it now:
            in the napalm storm of pain and shame,
            through the bloody mud of mucus and tears,
            over the clamp of knees upon my chest,
            his words snuck around the pound of fists:
                        I
                        hate
                        you
                        fucking
                        indians
            Through the thick curdle of fear
            I choked out what would be
            my first remembrance of qualified self-assertion:
                        but I'm a Mexican.

Unsure of himself, perhaps for the first time
that afternoon, he pulled back, sized me up,
picked over my features—chock of face, eye slant,

the plaster of black hair, the second-hand clothes.

His anger dispersed like a cloud of startled crows
steaming from a tree. He sorried himself,
picked me up. Told me that
he liked mexicans as he righted
his bike. Told me he thought that
I was an indian. That I was no good. However,
he knew some Mexicans at school
and they're OK. Did I know the Aguilars?

I wiped the blood on my shirt. I choked the tears
into a pit just below my throat. I looked straight ahead
as he walked me just within eyeshot
of our house on west Third. I felt the bruises
rise like fry marks on tortillas. He pedaled himself away,
straight through the bark of a chainlinked dog.

II. Later

you
   dumb
       caca,
my uncle would say a few days later
             now
               he knows
                    where you live.
A wasted threat, since I would say nothing, since I
would remain dumb as the dead. Silence without
irony, like a coin of tin under my tongue,
silence in the space of breath between laughter,
on the tip of finger suddenly pressing
the back of my throat when, weeks later,
first grade having been swallowed by summer,
I spotted him among the slap and splash
of the local public pool—brown freckles marring
the pink of his shoulders, a blinding shimmer
of chlorine and water, the concrete whitewashed
to a blistering brilliance.

Edwin Torres

MOTHER TONGUE: UNMAN CHANT

the tin-tin-tin follows
ca-*tuun-tuun* - *cata*-TAN
and I see myself
in the space
between the hits
    it's not
    how fast I play - it's not
    my speed
    no eastern notation
    no western idealism
how I hear
is where I place myself
before the - *caTUUN* - comes down -
piri - piri - piri - pown - skirts around the beat
before the beat
comes down surrounding every sound I found
myself inna place
where I laughed at familiar *off*
    and I know off so well
    I breathe its edge so good
    when I smell its presence it goes
    through my pores, through blood - traveling...
        gouging out river-*POW! pam-pam*
        para-po / para-po! CHAM!
          CHEEEEEEEI or no!
            Ga Tho ------------
            Ga Tho ------------
            GARA PA or no!
timbale to my bone
stirring slow familiar home
salsero to the beat
the one I come from - street but
street I be
tho' not in me - I pray these knees
my bended pleas - to hear me I - tho' lost...
        would stray inside you any day... / *bata-shun!*
          oron - oh no!

sal sorro - no...soy yo / de tu...this
thing I know - so well...I don't
mother tongue who fails me so
mother tongue inside me - YO!
mami ton son - suro no AYYY!
mama cuun-CON torro soy...san -
gre de...san - gre tuyo - pero no! ...I know

no hay SÓN puro de YO...
no pure song...of me...
no tongue...of you...
I am no where I know - where?
where I can be solo *BORI-coro*
de mi... AIY - AIY - Yoooooo / CO-RO
YAI - YAI - Yoooooo / ROYO
NO - NO - Yorro Mas
No Man No / Know Me? No,
No Soy Yo...

a man once unmanned
will man what is man
but once he is manned
a man will unman

me llamo Llame-e-e-e-e-e
un hombre sin nombre
me llama Llame-e-e-e-e-e
y ahora soy hombre

i live as a ma-a-a-a-n
a man of no name
my name is Unma-a-a-a-a-n
unman i remain

Oscar Mireles

LOST AND FOUND LANGUAGE

It started in 1949, when my oldest brother
came home from school
in Racine, Wisconsin
after flunking kindergarten
because he "spoke no English"
and declared to my parents
that "the rest of the kids have to learn to speak English
if we planned on staying here in the United States."

so my parents lined up
the rest of the seven younger children
had us straighten up
tilt our heads back
reached in our mouth with their hands
and took turns
slicing our tongues in half

making a simple, but unspoken contract
that from then on
the parents would speak Spanish
and the children would respond
back only in English

How do you lose a native language?
does it get misplaced
in the recesses of your brain?
or does it never quite stick to the sides
of your mind?

for me it would always start
with the question
from a brown faced stranger
"¿Hablas español?"
which means
"Do you speak Spanish?"

which meant

if they had to ask me
if I spoke Spanish
this was not going to be a good start for
having a conversation...

my face would start to get flushed
with redness and before
I had a chance to stammer
the words
"I don't"

I could see it in their eyes
looking at my embarrassed face
searching for an answer
that they already knew

as I walked away
I know they were thinking
"Who is this guy?"
"How can he not speak his mother's tongue?"
"Where did he grow up anyways?"
"Doesn't he have any pride
in knowing who he is?"
or "Where he came from?"

I tried to reply,
but as the words in Spanish
floated down from my brain
they caught in my teeth,
the rocks of shame.
I spoke in half-tongue.

my future wife
taught me how
to speak Spanish
mainly
by being Colombian
and not speaking English

and I had already knew
the language of hands and love
which got me confident enough

to reach deep inside
myself
to find the beautiful sounds and latin rhythms
that laid deep within me

and although
I still feel my heart jump a beat
when someone asks "¿Hablas español?"
now the Spanish resonates within me
and echos back "Sí, y usted tambien?"

and today as I talk with the Spanish speaking students
in our school
they can not only feel my words
they can feel my warm heart
splash ancient Spanish sounds off
my native tongue
that has finally grown whole again.

Orlando Ricardo Menes

BUGARRONES

1

In Cuban slang un bugarrón is a man who sodomizes
other men—or boys—but doesn't see himself as homosexual.
No kissing, no touching, no sugaries of love. Muy macho,
bullring toro. His gay partner is un pajarito
who puts on false eyelashes & eau de perfume,
smokes menthol cigarettes, fasts to stay slim, depilates.
During carnaval he's a crazy girl who wiggles
in a macaw-colored rumbera costume, plumes of paradise
in his beehive wig. The boy el bugarrón seduces is
always prepubescent. No pubic hairs, voice of a girl,
buttocks like clay before it's been fired in the kiln.

2

Bugarrón is not in any dictionary, perhaps some boogaloo
neologism from the tropics, Antillean in-your-face
chusma argot? The word bears a resemblance
to the British bugger, derived from Medieval Latin Bulgarus,
literally a Bulgarian, term of contempt for eleventh-century
heretics of that nation. Sodomy = heresy? Monks who
secretly worshiped Priapus and practiced fellatio ritualistically?
Te Deum orgies? Evangelium of men who love boys?
Cubans probably first heard bugger from English sailors
when a British fleet captured La Habana two centuries ago.
Most buggerers escaped punishment, for muleques (African-born
slaveboys) were abundant in the taverns & brothels
along the rocky waterfront. The violated boys would cower
in the stables of convents, whimpering & putting poultices
of horse-pissed straw on their backsides, their only succor
a cross of kindling sticks, pidgin prayers to Nuestra Señora
de la Leche whose breasts lactate mercies, abundant as rain.

3

Would bugarrones confess to being perverts?
Can the word even be translated to pederasty?
The Cuban male is either macho or pajarito,
the object of penetration irrelevant to his sexuality.
In this sense we are closer to the ancient Greeks
than to Anglos, though Socrates did not shame
any youth, barbarian or Greek, inserting the penis
between the boy's legs, intercrural position.
Who in our history might have been bugarrones?
Patriots? Soldiers? Martyrs? Our Founding Fathers
José Martí, Antonio Maceo, Carlos Manuel de Cespedes?
I should pause, retract my words. Political poems
are risky, sexual-political poems riskier still.

On the radio politicians incite exiles to take
revenge on the blasphemer. "Los machos
de la patria are sacred, tooth for a tooth, eye for an eye."
I hear them banging like men of Sodom
at Lot's door, one they call Ángel clutches
my hair, thrashes my body in dirt, muchachos tear
off my clothes, kick genitals. I taste salt
of their sweat, hear fury's soft wheezing.
This procession de repudio drags me
several blocks, Badia Restaurant to Bay of Pigs
memorial. Feet stomp like claves, shouts of maricón
rumbas. At the martyrs' burning flame,
Ángel rolls my words into a phallus, I swallow
them hard as the setting sun tints
our skies guava red.

Elizabeth Pérez

FOUND IN TRANSLATION

> *Thus the immediate consequence of their sin*
> *was that they had to begin sewing.*
> Midrash Rabbah-Genesis 19:6

"Do the dead want candles?"
was my mother's way of saying *yes.*
Cuban music escaped from the guitar-case of her mouth
as if to flee the flies, flannel hems, spooled dread,
and leap from smashed transom
to the one fruit-branched peach
where she grew three-piece suits
in the no-collar South.
            She earned rent and boiled tuber stitch by stitch.
Her way of saying *get out of bed:*
"You slept until your navel became a breast!"
Her sweat ransomed sons from factory's clutch;
while they ate sweet paste and glued mobiles in class,
zipper-teeth bit the frayed waist of the dress
where an island-shaped patch stanched
the mess at her ribs. Her Spanish freed
what the timecards trapped.
            Her father also made his way by saying,
made a pincushion of his tongue and a minimal wage.
Eight fingers smarting thimble-less
for payslips embossed with a lace baron's face,
he would call down the aisles of worsted lapels
at the decibel of twin girls, or tripped alarms:
"Recall the eye of the needle
through which we've passed!"
            And this: the softest hand has nails to scratch.

Liliana Valenzuela

NOV. 2, 1998,
ON THE EVE OF BECOMING AN AMERICAN CITIZEN

Not me, not I
a gringa I would never be
gritos de "muera el imperialismo yanqui"
resonando en mi cabeza
yo, la Malinche,
"there is always me-search in research"
going full circle
me an American
a Mexican-American
a bona fide Chicana chayote-head
My life is here now
raising my bilingual chilpayates
married, metida hasta las chanclas
in this brave new world.

A binational
una Nutella bicolor
vainilla y chocolate
dual citizenship, at least,
los políticos en México finally woke up
to us "raza" on this side of the border.
Welcome Paisano, Bienvenido Amigo,
hasta que se les prendió el foco, cabrones.
Ahora sí, pásenle, que su nopal está lleno de tunas.

Aquí en la frontera, en el no-man's-land,
mujer puente, mujer frontera,
mujer Malinche.

Ahora sí, cuando me chiflen por la calle
me podrán decir "gringuita" y por primera vez
lo seré, una bolilla, una gabacha,
mis ojos azules y cabello rubio por fin
corresponderán a los estereotipos de la gente
"But you don't look Mexican"
Enton's ¿qué parezco? ¿acaso tengo changos en la cara?

When I die, spread my ashes along the Rio Grande, the Río Bravo, where I once swam naked.

Lorena Duarte

WHO CARES ABOUT AMERICAN POETS?

who cares about American poets?
about our sufferings of pen and bleedings in ink,
about our dramatic and clichéd lines (see above),
about our improvised lives and ever ready to suffer smiles?

we've run out of things to say.
I think about four or five known wars and
many dozen secret wars ago
that last bit of such an oodling pastime as poetry was lost.

now, people want Bible "truth" or
perhaps are agnostically indifferent
or are numbed out television dumb
who knows?

point is, no one here reads poetry
and I'm not even really crazy about it
like NO ONE HERE DAMN THEM
but just like,
no one here reads poetry.
only other poem makers care to
figure out the tortured meaning of one
seamless phrase or another.

see, I am trying to write a
sestina, but I keep wondering why.

I suppose if it is an audience I want,
I should bill myself in my Latina poet way.
code-switch
y hablar about my the blood dancing in my veins,
mi pobre mama,
and how I don't care una mierda what anyone thinks.

pawn that identity of mine.

or perhaps join some scene —

but see, in the spoken word circles
it sounds so much better if it
has rhythm, rhymes,
makes you laugh
and screams "momma!"
and there they want me to tell
my brown woman story
the brown woman story
that brown woman story
and then <<sing>> just a little,
especially at the end.

and I don't sing.

then my terribly erudite friends
want abstractions and
associative logic and
white peacocks* and
green fuse driving flowers **
and believe me, so do I —

but how can I pour my
love and heartsweat over my
perfect "impromptus."
analyze every comma, dash,
adjective I use —

how? while the world turns to shit
and my dinner burns to a crisp?

I mean you want abstractions,
I can give you abstractions:
fiery webs I loop
in bitter clumps over
deaf deaf ears.

but anyway, is it just a big
masturbatory display?
acumen of words here on display!

she speaks—in two tongues!
and can approximate worthwhile

entertainment.

then of course, there are the ones who ask
what do you want this to do?
what is the point?
excellent question.

what also is the point of blade of grass or tree?

point is this—have you ever
heard a man cry like that?
have you ever made a man cry like that?
have you ever seen a flower so pretty,
had such a shitty day,
had such a funny thought?

you have? me too.

that's it.

the real question, I think,
should be something like,
and so? how does anything change?

I say it doesn't.

because no one here reads American poets.

there are no ears, no forums
for our want-to-be-blinding words.

and so, I think,
we run out of things to say.

* "He loved three things", *Poem Without a Hero and Selected Poems*, Anna Akhmatova.
** "The Force Through the Green Fuse Drives the Flower", Collected Poems, Dylan Thomas.

Paul Martinez Pompa

COMMERCIAL BREAK

Are your images inefficient?
Does your diction feel bland?
Are you tired of writing poetry
that simply does not work?

If you answered *yes* to any of these questions,
consider what a Mexican can do for you.
Strategically placed, a Mexican will stimulate
and fire up your drab, white poem.

Here at Pretty White Poetry,
we have an inventory of Mexicans
in all shades of brown.
Need an authentic-indigenous tone?
Try our mud-brown, Indian Mexican.

Your audience will taste the lust
in Montezuma's loins as they devour
your poem. Want a little spice
but not too much pepper?
A pale-brown, Spanish concentrated
Mexican is the perfect touch.

Maria, tortilla, mango, trabajo—
just a sample of the hundreds of exotic
words on sale waiting to decorate
your lines. Even Hispanic poets sprinkle
our Latin Lingo into their writing.
If our selection brings authenticity
to their work, imagine what it can do for yours!

Just listen to what happens to the following
lines after being pumped with a little Español:

Before it's—
    Grandma at the stove.

The open window pulls
bacon & eggs
smell to my nose
as I pass the house.

And after it's—
Abuelita at the comal, her skin
like café con leche. The open
window pulls huevos
con chorizo to my nose
as I pass the casita.

Pretty White Poetry understands the difficulty
of crafting well-paced rhythmic lines.
So we've imported Salsa-smooth
Puerto Rican vernacular* to make your diction
dance and your syntax sway.
Don't worry about mixing Mexican
and Puerto Rican imagery—
most of your readers won't know the difference!

Trouble with line breaks?
Our Mexicans specialize
in knowing exactly where it's safe
to break a line. After all, that's how some
got into the country in the first place!

Pretty White Poetry deals exclusively with docile,
safe language. Our words are edgy,
but never make liberal white readers uncomfortable—
that means more publishing opportunities for you!

And our Mexicans are cheap,
but they are always high-quality.
For here at PWP, our motto is:
"If your poem has Mexicans,
you know it's gonna work!"

*Puerto Rican vernacular available only while supplies last.

raúlrsalinas

LOUD AND PROUD

In loud voices we must sing.
Cantaremos porque...
Silence means consent.
Cantaremos porque...
Silence equals death.
If i am free to express my ways
then what i have to say
to this here nation state is,
don't spew me with hate.
Don't play that un-american card
with me pard-ner
because continentally speaking,
i am what i am!
No need for nationalistic,
Jingoistic, patriotic pap.
Remember world war II?
"We're gonna' have to slap
the dirty little jap,
and uncle sam's the guy who can do it."

In proud voice entonces
let me exercise my rights
---aboriginal and otherwise---
As we grieve one more time
for those who gave up the spirit on 9/11
now gone to their heaven.
30 years we've been grieving,
weaving our tears
into spears of struggle.
Feel las voces of the poets in the wind!
Listen to the singing of artistas
on communal walls!
See la música splash
rainbows on our souls!

Loud and proud
i sing

my ritmos and rimes
in these times
of patriotismo gone astray
disgusting display
bustin' out all over town;
including the brown.
Flying of the flags
used to disguise body bags
that carried medal of honor winners
back to hick towns of
coffee-serving refusals
& cemetery of heroes burial denials.

In proud voices
we will sing.
So with all due respect to my Mom
and her need to fly a flag
for her man
who fought in some other war,
wrap me not in waving rags
that gag the wailing
of the masses en Acteal.
Irlandeses both protestants and catholics
their paths plowed under/Lebanon plundered
and as the colony crumbles
Palestine rumbles,
Intifada!

In loud voices
we shall sing
though the empire is
in shambles
cantaremos
of the niños mutilados
en Irak,
Atenco,
and Kabul,
Rolando en Vieques;
yanqui doodle
contaminación.
La liberación de los pueblos,
we must sing.

Loud and proud
cantaremos
lift our voice
that one collective
and united
voz
must not be stilled.
Strong-willed seguiremos
cantaremos
we must sing,
we will sing!
Bringing to our
gente decente
that other realidad.

Minneapolis, MN
September 2006

PROSE
FICTION, CREATIVE NON-FICTION, TESTIMONIOS & ESSAYS

Aureliano Maria DeSoto

A QUERENCIA OF ONE'S OWN

Recently playing on US Spanish-language television stations has been a series of advertisements hawking language tapes, compact discs, and DVDs that promise to teach immigrants how to speak English with proficiency and ease. Typically constructed around a series of before and after vignettes as subtle as Eisenstein's Soviet flapper whose life has been made much easier with the introduction of a automated milking machine for the collective in *The Old and the New*, the before of degrading and embarrassing uniligualism is visually contrasted with the utopian after of the new, better-dressed, fully functional and empowered bilingual Latinas and Latinos. As a commercial mechanism, this is a not a terribly innovative strategy. However, one element of the advertisement has remained stuck in my head. As maids and laborers turn magically into white collar workers on the screen, the voice over narration insists, logically, that this is so because, "El exito está escrito en inglés!" The advertisements reinforce the simplistic notion that assimilation is just a matter of speaking English; that is, the only important difference between Americans (successful because they speak English) and Latina/o immigrants (losers unable to speak English) is solely and exclusively language, and not deep cultural, social, economic, and political differences.

Linguistic assimilation into English as a mode to socio-economic success and stability is such a truism for new Latino immigrants that these commercials can explicitly use the fantasy of English language proficiency as a pathway to middle-class comfort to sell its product. The irony of these commercial advertisements is that they play on this deeply held belief among new Latino immigrants that does not seem to have been disabused by the evidence of lots of disempowered and fully anglophone US Latinas/os around them. For many anglophone US Latinas/os, our place within English has not generally, in and of itself, extended the social, cultural, and economic homeland that immigrants pursue. If anything, language assimilation for US Latinas/os has been and remains a process of ambivalence.

Growing up in Los Angeles in the seventies and eighties, I felt the weight and power of anti-Mexican sentiment. Spanish, as the language indelibly associated with the mass of Latin American laborers, service workers, and others at the bottom of the economic pile, became intertwined with the racist and classist assumptions of my social space, which was interestingly enough divorced from my immediate experience of familial and neighborhood networks. What was known intimately was left behind, and for many years I had a powerful aversion to learning Spanish fluently. It wasn't until many years living away from Los Angeles, and in the emotional embrace of my Latin American partner, that I could begin again to approach the tapestry of Spanish free from the painful and embarrassed associations I had attached to the language as a child and teenager.

My experience in American school was marked by this linguistic repulsion. My family was remarkably assimilationist, so I entered school relatively capable in petit bourgeois English. While I grew up surrounded by the sound of Spanish daily within the household, and my grandparents were fully fluent, my family was not unaware of the obvious advantages to a primarily anglophone linguistic identity. Yet, even given my proficiency in English, I was marked both by the narrow assumptions of educational administrators who constantly watched my performance because I came from a Spanish-speaking household. This reached a zenith (or perhaps nadir) when, in the tenth grade, in my eleventh year of formal anglophone education, I was called into the ESL office to take a language ability test. The test was composed of pictures of the developing world, which I was asked to describe verbally. It was quickly clear to both the administrator and myself the ridiculous nature of this examination, yet oddly, the examination was required to run a course, and I spent at least thirty minutes describing pictures to an embarrassed teacher. This is one instance of official discourses of difference that always formed a backdrop, like white noise, to my educational experience. At the time, I experienced Los Angeles as a deeply racist place, where Mexicans formed the official underclass of workers, cleaners, janitors, and disempowered ones: a nameless, faceless mass of dissuasion. And the language of this mass was Spanish. Given the racist assumptions of the society around me, I made my choices accordingly.

However, the best way I can describe these experiences is through the lens of ambivalence. In most cases, it is only retrospectively that we can afford the luxury of political consciousness, and I was no different. I made choices that were determined by the society I was a member of, but I did not see my decisions in purely instrumental terms. For me, my identity as an English-speaking Latino was a site of euphoria. I was a participant in anglophone music and pop culture subcultures that went beyond the US, and felt connected linguistically to British, Australian, and Asian and African English-speaking expressions that I recognized as remarkably different from those of my Spanish-speaking cohort, family, and neighbors. While the Spanish door was closed, temporarily, the English one opened, beckoning me to a world where I could be recognized differently, outside of my lackluster public high school and working class neighborhood of single-family homes, taquerias and burger stands. In this sense, language was indelibly associated with class, and as this was the eighties, I followed that pathway to success with relish, both pushed out of Spanish by racism and classism and drawn into English by the seduction of achievement. El exito está escrito en inglés, indeed!

And here is the crux, as they say, of the matter. Only in retrospect can most of us afford a critical political consciousness, and children make decisions in order to survive. The weight of these decisions can become difficult to account for with the development of a more critical perspective. For Latina/o intellectuals, the power of the choices we have made to repress Spanish in favor of English is evident in the success we find ourselves having attained. We communicate in the Anglo language we have made ours, yet this is an awkward fit. If we are evidently brown skinned, articulate speech marks us in complicated ways for both Anglos and other Latinos. This is made even worse if we are unilingually anglophone. If we are light-skinned enough to pass as a white American, the disconnect between our physical selves, manner of presentation, and facility with the English language can cause discomfort when others attempt to place us within categories of identity. In both cases, Latinas/os and other Americans of different racial backgrounds inscribe language and culture onto the body in narrow ways that speak both to the big socio-political agendas (race, nationalism, identity) and individual knowledges based in the familial and familiar. What does a Latina/o look like? What sound do we expect to emerge from the mouth of this particular vision? When that expectation is not met, we are disoriented. The phrase "You speak English so well" is not one I have ever heard directed at me, but the implication seems to be always present.

My impression is that the strong association between class and language that typified my childhood and adolescence has not changed terribly, even though arguably Los Angeles and the United States are very different places now. For those US Latinos who have developed English proficiency, especially the intellectual class of cultural producers, writers, and academics, the tension between the racist and assimilationist forces which drove us to English are mired in a deep ambivalence about ourselves as present yet absent in the nomenclature of "America." In some ways, the Latina/o intellectual wears the anxiety about personal choices to succeed in the language of Anglo-America on his or her sleeve. This is why we insist on testing each other on the field of language, for language represents for us painful choices, pointed memories, and personal investments in how these complicated histories should figure in our ideal political utopias of adulthood. To these ends, we politicize language and its uses in ways that strike Latin Americans as ridiculous. We test each other, measuring each other's depths through the use of Spanish, always with an invisible question mark at the end: how Latino are you, exactly?

The opening greeting or dropped phrase in Spanish, unless by previous agreement or acquaintance, is a loaded weapon. And the response to the challenge is always already political. I suppose some brave souls who actually speak little or no Spanish could reply that they don't understand, however given that these moments are rarely about actual comprehension and linguistic facility, this is not usually the tack. Respond in English, and you are making a decisive break in the implicit dialogue: I will not participate in this game with you. This can be friendly or defensive. If one chooses to respond in Spanish, other things are at play: accent, intonation, and phraseology. When I was more unilingually anglophone, I would prefer the former method. I always felt that there was an implicit value being placed on the response. What kind of Latino are you? Down with la causa, a peninsular pretender, or an assimilationist? Invariably, the sites for these tests were English-speaking professional or social spaces, often in the presence of unilingual non-Latino anglophones. Now that I am more bilingual, I am not intimidated so much by these questions. I can respond fluently, make idle conversation, funny asides. My experiences as an adult have removed Spanish from the realm of the culturally significant, in the sense that Spanish has become a language of quotidian discourse. After all, every day millions of people begin their day and go to sleep having spoken only Spanish, a fact completely unremarkable to them. Spanish for them, and increasingly for me, is just another language in a world full of them, apolitical in and of itself.

Yet, so often it seems as if some essential quality of latinidad is grounded in language. For Anglos and Latinos alike, linguistic ability in Spanish appears as the basis from which identity springs. Given the wide diversity of language ability among US Latinas/os, the impression that Spanish is the touchstone of the Latina/o soul seems both a powerful tool against anglophone assimilation as well as a fantastical projection of cultural authenticity as opposed to our quotidian, mongrel, assimilated selves. Many of us, even if not fully bilingual, grew up around the sounds of Spanish, and the warm notes of the language can trigger the deepest, most intimate memories. Yet for the most part, Latinos beyond the second generation are more fluent, and tend to be more comfortable, in English, reflecting both the place where we live and the varying experiences we have had within an anglophone educational system that divorces us from Spanish.

Language in all its myriad manifestations political, social, or otherwise, is a lightening rod for US Latinas/os. No matter the extent to which we remove ourselves from Spanish, it constantly reasserts itself, bubbling up in unexpected ways as the return of the repressed: racism, exclusion, painful difference, as well as love, belonging, communitas, and expression. Brimming over with implicit political, social, and cultural meaning, the debate over language among Latinos in the USA remains a central co-nundrum for many reasons. The multi-generational and continual structure of Latino immigration means that Latinos as a social group can never attain a fully assimilated post-immigration "eth-nic" group. Racism and xenophobia prevent even assimilated La-tinas and Latinos from comfortably assuming American identity completely. Like myself, for many Latinas/os formal education is the linchpin of language consciousness, and with good reason, for school is where the prescribed mechanisms of English-speak-ing American society meet and subsequently constrain the poly-glot experiences of Latinas/os. The extent to which school and the linguistic terrors of education are powerful tropes of Latina/o consciousness is revealed by the pitched battles over the use value and long-term effects of anglophone assimilation for Latino schoolchildren, not only in discussions of programs like bilingual education but in the larger question of the intentions of formal education for the Latina/o child.

Along a political trajectory, rightists tend to insist on the necessity of this process, while leftists seek some compromise through cultural or linguistic preservation. Yet, away from the printed page, journals, and conference panels that seek to em-pirically measure this intangible, my impression is that Latina/o schoolchildren negotiate this polemical dyad in complex ways. The anglophone classroom reveals the terror of Latina/o linguistic differences that are embedded in much larger discourses about national, social, cultural, and ethnic belonging. However, at the same time that Latinas/os are continually compelled to imbibe the dominant culture through lesson plans, instructional measurement, and peer pressure, it would be a mistake to label such a process exclusively coercive. English holds the promise of greater socio-economic empowerment for new Latina/o immigrants, as well as opening the diverse world of global anglophone popular culture expression, which after all is much more than just racist Anglo American mores and values.

What we seem to be looking for in our collective and individual debates on language and Latina/o identity is a sort of querencia, a home place that we have an innate sense of being from and constantly returning to. The word querencia has roots in querer, to love, but also refers to the pen a bull retreats to when wounded during a bullfight. This dimension of combat and retreat to a safe space is what gives the word its sophisticated nuance, and what also makes it apropos to the situation of Latinas/os and the battleground language represents. For many of us, Spanish forms a utopian diasporic querencia, where our true soul lives, whether that be emotional, cultural, or truly linguistic.

But a complementary perspective might be to try and begin imagining English as an alternative linguistic *querencia*, one much more quotidian for US Latinas/os but in that sense more tangible as well. One of the most compelling aspects of contemporary Latina/o immigration to the United States has been the extent to which our presence affects and transforms the Anglo-American state and connects it more broadly to the larger hemisphere, often times kicking and screaming every step of the way. This should not be understood as a didactic, black-and-white process of reaffirming anglophone roots and traditions versus a creeping corruption from the Spanish-speaking south, or alternatively, preserving ourselves as Latin American cultural actors preserved in aspic. Both of these models are museum pieces, frozen in time and space.

Instead, a complicated and symbiotic new linguistic organism is emerging that affects not only anglophone Americans and US Latinos, but also the citizens of America latina. What is emerging is an unpredictable spectrum of linguistic and social identifications that coexist with and within each other rather than jostle for paradigmatic supremacy. For myself and other anglophone Latinas/os, the real challenge, and our potential power, is claiming a stake in the future of English as a global language. In this sense, while our ambivalent identities may pine for Spanish as the language of the Latin soul, we are building new, more durable querencias within the language of English.

Ana M. Lara

A CHANGE OF MANTA, SANTO DOMINGO, 2004

Weaving a New Manta to Live By:

I recently had a crisis of conscience. And within this crisis, I learned many lessons which I will happily share with you today in the hopes that you will walk away with something new for your life.

Let's get the credentials out of the way, shall we?

I am truth teller, I am a seer, I am a healer, a curandera. Trained in the traditions of dreams and ancestors. I am an organizer, an artist and a writer in spirit. I am an anthropologist by degree and public health snuck in there, too. I am an omnivore, a woman, a Jew, a lesbian. I am black, Latina, American, Dominican, and a global nomad. I am of Africa, I am of Europe, I am of America. I am a child of communists turned technocrats, intellectuals with dashed dreams. This is my last life on this planet: and yes, I believe in re-incarnation.

The first question I ask is how we can deal with the limitations of the languages that we already have. The answer that comes to mind is two-fold. The first fold is about my ancestral lineages, truths and messages. The second fold is about the application of those truths to my current reality.

I didn't always know about my ancestors. They were hidden in layers of family secrets, or stored away in my aunt's basement waiting for the dust to be blown off of their captured images. Some of them have no graves to speak of, and others are set in beds of stone, concrete and stainless steel.

I first learned about my ancestors through my name. It's an ancestral name, of sorts. It's Ana-Maurine Higginbotham Lara. **Ana** because it's easy to pronounce if you know how to pronounce it. Ana because it's in Spanish, with one "n". Ana, as in Anacaona - the female Taino leader who resisted the Spanish colonizers. **Maurine** because it's my maternal grandmother's name. With a French spelling because either she liked French or there were some French people in the mix. **Higginbotham**. A proper English name, the name of my maternal grandfather. It's the name that connects me to slavery through the legacy of slave owners, and freed blacks in the United States. And **Lara**, the name of my paternal great-grandfather, a farmer, a mulatto, a descendent of a Spanish man and a faceless black woman.

I then learned about my ancestors through story-telling. Over the dinner table, at family gatherings, through the laughter of familial jokes and memories. Through the tears raised by another one's death. I learned that Aunt Mattie was a painter. I learned that Don Enrique won the lottery. I learned that after we had been here for several hundred years, working the land that belonged to others, my family finally lived on some of their own. And that ironically enough: it had a gold mine on it. The gold that brought us to this land in the first place.

I learned that my family has struggled to wrap Spanish words into meaning, until it is the only language in which they dream. I learned that the new generation born in the United States has swapped Spanish for a more pertinent colonizer's tongue: English. I learned that my American family has always dreamt in English, with a little Irish and German along the way. That they have no need to look for other tongues, because after all, it is their dream that has become reality.

I have applied this knowledge, these truths, and the power of these lineages in creating my current reality. I wrap myself in my ancestor's stories. I look at their photographs, I search for compassion in myself to forgive them for what they have done. They have made it possible for me to be here today, and in recognition of this, I use their lives as lessons. All of what I learn and apply comes from places where spoken language only sometimes serves as a medium of interpretation. More often, my lessons come in images, in visions, in dances and rituals.

The second question that came out of my crisis is how we develop new language with which to interact. Especially given that language can only go so far. How do we create new ways of interacting and speaking with one another? I don't have the answer to this question, but I do have some thoughts.

When we are stripped, naked, to our core we are left with the lowest common denominators: our vulnerabilities, our bodies, our ability to see, hear, touch, taste, smell and remember. We are forced to confront our fears about being in the world. I believe that the answer to creating new ways of interacting with each other is being able to get down to that place of absolute vulnerability, and re-discovering our bodies and senses. Remembering what it feels like to taste, touch, smell, hear and see. It is in this state that we can begin to see the shields that have been welded onto us through the development of social constructs. It is where we can begin to understand the role and place of ancestral knowledge in teaching us new ways (that are really old ways).

Example #1: The world was not always made of rational thought. It still isn't.

Example #2: Some of us have the genitals of both sexes, the spirit of both genders.

Example #3: There are molasses colored people on every continent, and we have all different kinds of features. The only thing we have in common is the caramel tones of our flesh.

Example #4: A blind man has to rely on his ears.

Example #5: Whiteness only adheres to the ones who believe it has power.

Example #6: All societies invent new languages when the ones they have aren't enough, such as Spanglish, Kreyol...and English.

The third and final question that arose out of my crisis was: at the end of the day, who are our people? And why is this question still relevant in 2004?

As an organizer, I can find a million reasons why it's still relevant. It's still relevant because there are people in jail right now who have not had fair trials. It's still relevant because WIC is about to disappear. It is still relevant because this morning there was another homicide. It is still relevant because some people are gathering their people to create a social project where my people suffer. It is still relevant because my people participate in this social project, knowingly and unknowingly.

As a healer, I find that I cannot answer this question. Because my role is to heal those who come to me, regardless of where they have been. It is in my role as a healer that social constructs have no relevance. It is in my role in dealing with peoples' bodies, spirits and emotional and intellectual vulnerabilities that I have to exercise the highest discipline to do the healing work. And because my ancestor's stories are complex, and because their stories are realized in my flesh: my lips, my eyes, my skin, my laugh, my ears, my walk, my illnesses and gifts, I am often forced to relinquish this question of who are our people. The only answer I have for sure is in their stories.

Because it's what I've always worn

I have recently had a crisis of conscience. It happened about three years ago when I moved to California and lost my Latina identity. That is, very few people out there saw me as Latina. It was the first time in my life I had been stripped of something that I thought was inherent. They took one look at my black skin, my mulatta features, my curly hair. They listened to me speak, a funny kinda speak...like that of somewhere else, and figured I was an African-American woman who had learned to speak Spanish. Who is they, you ask? The people I had believed I had some inherent connection to: The Chicanos, Mexicanos of Aztlan. The centroamericanos of San Francisco. The mainlanders.

Not to say there aren't black people in Mexico: there are and they are a vibrant, thriving set of communities, but largely unrecognized by the Mexican media, and other entities such as, oh I don't know: Univision. One would think that with the large number of Puerto Ricans and Cubans that perhaps invisibility wouldn't happen so much, but I was very shocked to find that it did. Again, and again, and again. Even though everyone and their mothers was dancing salsa and merengue, and drinking mojitos, I was an invisible Latina. Strange, isn't it?

I made a point of reaching out to all the Latino youth who passed by me. And on the other side of the equation, I was left scrunching my nose in the Dominican gesture signifying "what?" many times when a young vato would come out with his mexicano influenced slang" Orale huey.." A slang that was Total Street, a slang that was parallel to anything any tigre in the streets of Santo Domingo would rival with his hand slap, head gestures and eye cutting look: "Dime." he would say, response: a sucking of teeth, a quick and subtle head movement. "Na'a." Yet, while I can understand any gesture thrown my way, I had no clue what the vatos were saying for months.

So I had a crisis of conscience. I am not an immigrant to the United States. Even weirder still. My mom is a U.S. citizen by birth, rubia, blonde anglo-saxon protestant. Look up WASP in the dictionary there's a picture of my mother. I was born in Santo Domingo, land of coincidences and crossroads. My father is Afro-Dominican, though his passport reads trigueño. He's never immigrated to the United States. I didn't live out my childhood in the States. I grew up in Africa. And after six months in Israel, and four years at the Jewish Y in Mount Vernon New York, I converted to Judaism when I was in high school and college. Yeah - there's the college stuff, too.

Of course, this story so far doesn't include my extended family: about thirty people that came to the U.S. after standing in long lines for visas outside the American consulate on Maximo Gomez in La Capital. They came and settled in a four block area of Adams Morgan, before it was gentrified. That is, in the 1960s. And then again in the 1990s. Yeah: and I have two cousins in NYC — the Bronx and alphabet city. And some straggling remnants of family in the Capital: Santo Domingo. You ask them if they're Latino. They'll tell you their Dominican. You ask them if they are black, and they'll tell you you're crazy. They want nothing to do with the quotas that the US imposed on Haitian immigrants.

I'm in the Dominican Republic right now for about six months. The other day I was speaking with a Dominican girl whom I was befriending. After I explained to her that in certain parts of the United States (if not all) I am considered black, I watched her eyebrows go up as she exclaimed, "but you're not black!" She's darker than me, straightens her hair and has streaked it with blonde highlights. My hair is locked, much to the dismay of many in my family— simply because they are convinced by something other than 30 years of black pride that I have "good hair". My new friend was thinking similar thoughts. I shook my head, thinking about whether to intercept with some consciousness raising, or listen to what she's thinking. I listened. She said to me, "Look, we're descendents of Spaniards and Africans. There's very little Indian. So we're mostly Spanish and African. But, I'm racist. Against Haitians, that is." Why? I asked. She said, "Well, I wasn't alive for those 22 years of occupation, but I am angry that they occupied this country. I think they are trying to take over the island. They are trying to take over our country. And I don't like the way they walk." I pointed out gently, after all we were still forming a friendship, that Haiti doesn't have the resources for a takeover. And that it's not Haitian franchises I see popping up all over the country. That is unless Pizza Hut, Pepsi, Coca Cola, Wendy's, McDonalds, Burger King, Baskin Robbins, Haagen Dazs, Hilton, Verizon, Hollywood Cinemas, Outback Grill and all the "free trade zones" are Haitian and I just didn't know.

Let's focus on some history: social history, not personal history. I am thinking about 512 years of colonization. That is 512 years since the arrival of chaos in the guise of European traders. I am thinking of the year 1513...That is we are 10 years short of 500 when the first African slaves arrived to this very island on which I happened to be born. They were brought from Spain, first: ladinos, Christianized and speaking the traders' tongues. Then the Portuguese and the Dutch caught onto the capitalist potential and we were dragged here en masse, with the wicked blessings of African traders who didn't realize their 1500 years of golden civilization was about to end with their betrayals. Cimarrones...that's what they called the ones who ran away into the mountains of the island. Caciques...the tainos who led the way and used the caves to hide their presence. That is, the few families that remained.

The language of this half of the island is a battle between the ones who want to remember their glorious arrival, and the ones who resisted and continue to resist that as the only truth. That is, the wealthy and the poor. The written word is taught in schools, and less than 70% of the population gets past 6th grade, but somehow the government has stats that say 85% are literate. The government is lying. It's the spoken word that counts, the song, the music, the dance and the gestures. Someone giving their word is still respected in the campos, and stories are told between farming and cooking. It's the bachata that tells you the latest chismes. It's the merengues that get into the bones, causing babies, matrimonies and deaths. It's the hands flying through the air between cars, space and time that tell you what a woman is thinking, or what a man has left behind. Our bodies speak and say more than the books that most people cannot afford.

For the country's working and middle class, it's a psychological battle against Haiti, a desire to be as wealthy as the estadounidenses without being Puerto Rico. It's a desire to speak American English, because "it's practical", and a complete neglect of Kreyol. It's a battle to hide the English of the sugar plantations and of the northern city of Samaná, where black folks came over 100 years ago from Philly and North Carolina; their English is not allowed. It's a battle to hide the gestures of hips, lips and hands that connect us all in a web of history that speaks through our movement.

Let me give you some more history, local history. Nigua is 50 km outside of the capital city of Santo Domingo. A month ago they celebrated the day of the cimarron. It was raining, and the venue was the first sugar plantation of the European landing:

Ingenio Diego Colon in Boca de Nigua. Just 15 kilometres away was the center of the first maroon community in the Americas. The rain didn't matter. It's always rained. We just moved inside, under the eaves of the tin roof now covering the ovens where ancestors suffocated in the heat, and sugar cane juice boiled over into caramel. Our bodies moved in the darkness of another power outage. We celebrated with palos: drums, guiro and maracas. We celebrated it with son. We danced merengue, son and palos. Black bodies, mandingos and mulatos. A girl smiled as a young man leaned against the wall. A scarf flew through the darkness as shoulders shimmered in the damp air of rain. A man made a fist with his thumb out, pointing towards his mouth. I shook my index finger, no. I didn't want a drink.

The silent language of bodies moving, gestures signaling, drums hiding the true intentions of gatherings. That is the history to which I am tied. This is the history that speaks to me, to the ways I react to rain. The ways I react to rules and structure. None of this is demonstrated on Univision. None of this is considered in the Latino census. Black people are not considered in the Latino census. The indigenous people of this continent are also not considered. Salma Hayek and James Edward Olmos are supposed to be our face, our language, our identity. National organizations are supposed to speak to our needs and the biggest question is: Bilingual education. Excuse me?

Let's step back and speak in some other terms.

I went to a Latino caucus in 2002 at a **US national** conference of organizers and activists. Me and a black Panamian friend were almost barred from entering. Here is the transcript:

Woman at the Door: You are in the wrong place, this is the Latino caucus.

Me and Friend: Yes, we're Latino.

Woman: But, the caucus is in Spanish.

Me: I speak Spanish. [My friend stood silent, he doesn't speak Spanish. I thought to myself, where are the translators?]

Woman: Well, come in.

We walked in amongst the stares and whispers and sat down on the floor. Two male Mexicanos, migrant workers were talking about working as farm laborers and the issues raised by lack of documentation, changes in California laws and such. I felt the pain of their struggle because I saw everyday how the laborers stood in desperate lines on Cesar Chavez, waiting for a pick up truck to take them somewhere to work. But, I couldn't help but think about the connections between this struggle and the struggle of female garment workers on the east coast. I raised my hand: what about the garment workers? The women in the room stayed silent. I then asked, Are there translators? And the second generations? I was given the stares. I was told that to be a true Latino meant that you spoke Spanish. My friend winced behind me, I felt my face light up with anger. I was told I was out of place. For what, I asked. Being a woman, being black, being Caribbean or being young? Or is it that I demanded a multilingual space? To encompass the total reality of who we are in America? If that can even begin to encompass it.

And it's not just identity politics in the United States that I am talking about. In 1999, I went to the Latin American feminist conference in Santo Domingo, Dominican Republic. Where there were no translators for the 50 Brazilian women, 30 Haitian women and others who didn't speak Spanish as their primary language. For example: English, French, Kreyol, Patois, Papiamiento, Quechua...I, the daughter of a diplomat, fluent in four languages, translated in French, Portuguese, Spanish and English. I stood up with the Haitian women who demanded an end to hegemony, to racism within the ranks of feminism: and I translated from their French to Dominican Spanish. I did the same for the Brazilian women, who walked out and had to be led back in by my pleading hand. All of this in front of 2000 Spanish speaking Latin Americans.

If we look at the history of language in the Dominican Republic, for example, we see multiple examples of linguistic hegemony as a tool for oppression. 1) Kreyol was barred during the Trujillo dictatorship. Or if you spoke Spanish with the rolling r's of the French influence, "perejil" becomes "pelejil" and fuang - you were likely to be assassinated. 2) I have never seen a nation so quick to disown its own as I have seen Dominicans. For example, the idea that Spanglish is an outgrowth of the Dominican Yorks (Dominicans in New York), denigrated by the middle and upper classes for their working class ethics. "They are neither here nor there... them? They are not Dominican, they're dominican yorks..." Yet, every Dominican person who lives here knows that when a party esta "heavy" or "full", it means its good. 3) Your accent is your class. Your class is your nationality. Your nationality defines your rights. "No, pero ese es Haitiano." "Negro, nosotros na'ma tenemos indios." "Esos cocolos si hablan un español machaca'o."

The legacy of nationalism is alive and well in our use of language: it fosters insecurity around identity that leads to the creation of a strict, narrow definition of belonging. That is the legacy that I resist, and that I think it is necessary to resist if we are to deepen our analyses and complexities as peoples in the Western Hemisphere. It's the same legacy that is in place in the United States right now.

I have recently had a crisis of conscience. Whose agenda is the Latino agenda? What does it mean for me to be Latina? To have been born from a gringa and a Dominican, raised in Africa fluent in three tongues from childhood? What does it mean when the people I relate to in my country of birth want nothing to do with Spanish, or the Spanish history of dominance? Or when the extended family I was born into wants nothing to do with those same people, because my family made it over and those people are still on the island? What to do with the reactions when I point out in the context of US Latino spaces that not all people in Latin America have Spanish as their first language, that it's just not the truth. Or that nationalism is being reinforced by the development of a Latino identity, and nationalism is directly contrary to indigenous land rights, and the promotion of human rights for communities and individuals?

An acquaintance once asked me, many years ago, what makes a Latino? I tried to respond: language. She pointed out, "what about all the indigenous people on the continent? What about kreyol?" So I said, the common experience of immigration. She responded, "but not all Latinos emigrate. And not everyone who does immigrate identifies as Latino." Then I answered, our love of music and dance. She replied, "I'm from central america. The first time I saw someone gyrate their hips was from behind a window where I hid as the garifunas paraded by. Besides, my family is Evangelical," she said. "We don't dance or listen to music." That defeated my religion argument.

As part of my crisis, I have taken well to the stripping of my identity. Sure I was angry about it for awhile. I felt the petulant attitude of a child who is told they are too young to understand. But, as part of deepening my analysis, I had to let go of the manta "Latina" that used to cover my shoulders— it didn't fit me anymore. What I see as being Latino in the United States is not my struggle, and yet I am intricately tied to some of the realities that arise out of this homogenous political definition. An ally to immigrants from all nations, yes...as long as there are national borders, I will fight for the human rights of immigrants. An ally to poor people, everywhere: whether campesinos, Haitian laborers or garment workers, yes. I will go to the rallies, I will listen to our stories, and I will not let the violence that affects our lives go unchallenged. A believer in African-based resistance and Africanity, yes. The history of Africans on the American continent is complex and spans across all language and nations. An ally to indigenous rights without nationalism, yes. I don't tolerate racism among any peoples.

As most people in the world, I am a person of complex mixed cultural and ethnic identities that circumscribe narrow nationalist and racist definitions of purity and belonging. I have been educated in the United States, a fact which gives me access to English which then allows me to write this essay. A fact which has allowed me to access the ways in which many in my mother's nation of birth think, including those within academic institutions. I speak Spanish, and have spent much time in the Dominican Republic, the nation of my own birth and my father's origin: at least as far back as slavery. My Dominican Spanish also gives me access to how people think, and differentiates my experience from that of other Spanish speakers from throughout the continent. But both of these languages are the languages of Domination, Colonial History and European power. They don't begin to encompass the complexities of who I am, or who the people in Nigua are, or what our struggles have been.

Perhaps we need a new way of defining things; a new way to think about languages and identity. These questions, these thoughts, form the cloak that covers my shoulder, the manta that heals my wounds and that gives me the tools to live by. I have come to believe that if we are to come away with a complex understanding of how language has functioned in the lives of people born in the Americas, we have to confront the layers of complex histories, the silences, the blanks, the contradictions and the bleeding sores. We have to find the points of resistance and learn from them, we have to believe that they are relevant. We have to be stripped of everything we took for granted so that we can get to deeper truths. And we have to go to those places where language is just a medium for interpretation.

Teresa Nasarre

¡NO INGLEESH, NO INGLEESH!

Allí estaba, dando vueltas y vueltas por la terminal tras haberse tomado un par de sandwiches y varios cafés. En su impaciencia por llegar al aeropuerto, Isabel, había olvidado que los aviones siempre se retrasan. El gesto de fastidio que el hecho le provocaba no tardó, sin embargo, en desaparecer de su rostro. Pensaba en su madre, para quien aquél era ser su primer viaje en avión. Hacía más de un año que no la veía.

Isabel recordó su figura, recia y robusta, igual que una enorme gallina siempre dispuesta a defender a sus polluelos. Su naturaleza práctica, solo atenta a las necesidades más primarias de aquellos a los que quería. Fuerte y voluntariosa. Atada a la tierra, como la hembra de un toro.

Cuando su padre murió, ella sola, se hizo cargo de la pequeña tienda que tenían en el barrio consiguiendo sacarla a flote a pesar del golpe que supuso la apertura de dos grandes supermercados en la zona. Frente a los precios de sus competidores su madre ofrecía conversación. Los vecinos, refugiados bajo el manto de sus palabras, se relajaban, hablaban y sobre todo, compraban. Así consiguió llevar a la universidad a sus cinco hijos, aunque ella apenas hubiera ido a la escuela. Por un momento, a Isabel le pareció volver a sentir su voz. Su madre sabía dotar el discurso, cualquiera que éste fuese, de calor y vida.

Ahora, mientras miraba el panel con la información del vuelo que la traía de Madrid, cuando apenas faltaban unos minutos para que éste aterrizara, el rostro de Isabel volvió a contraerse en un gesto de tensa impaciencia. Esta vez no era el tiempo que llevaba esperando allí, en la terminal, sino todo lo que le rodeaba. New York, una ciudad de luces y rascacielos que adoraba pero también temía. Su nueva vida. Nuevo trabajo y nuevos amigos cuya lengua, ajena, les hacía extraños. Una vez disipado el encanto del descubrimiento, los días comenzaron a transcurrir al ritmo de lo cotidiano y sintió estar viviendo en un completo vacío. Más que nunca necesitaba escuchar español en la voz de su progenitora. Abrigo y calor. Por eso fue una sorpresa todo lo que ocurrió después.

Apenas su madre apareció, la sintió diferente. Aunque sus abrazos y besos tenían la misma fuerza de siempre, su mirada vagaba temerosa por los carteles que colgaban del aeropuerto debilitando su actitud. Isabel lo atribuyó al cansancio del viaje, pero al pedirle que se quedara un momento sola, junto al equipaje, mientras ella se acercaba al mostrador donde podían informarle del precio de los taxis, la mujer le agarró del brazo.

Su hija le aseguró que sería solo cuestión de un minuto y se alejó sin entender aquella reacción, hasta que hubo una avalancha de viajeros. Entonces, desde lejos, vio cómo un policía se dirigía a su madre. Simplemente le indicaba que dejara paso a algunos de ellos, los que iban en silla de ruedas, pero solo consiguió sobresaltar a la mujer que, sin reparar en la situación, comenzó a repetir con labios temblorosos.

- No *Ingleesh*, Yo no *Ingleesh*...

Isabel corrió hacia ella de nuevo.

- Mama, no te preocupes, no es nada.

Luego habló con el asombrado oficial — ...It´s OK, she doesn´t speak English... — y más tarde con el taxista — ...twenty one between first and second... — mientras su madre, acurrucada a su lado, parecia ir menguando en el asiento.

Súbitamente, la muchacha sintió que su vida entera desfilaba ante su mirada al mismo y caótico ritmo con el que la ciudad se sucedía tras la ventanilla del vehículo, dejando atrás un paisaje para atrapar otro nuevo que diera paso, a su vez, a otro y a otro. De alguna manera supo que su destino se había puesto en marcha, que había crecido y que iba—ya no tenía miedo—a seguir haciéndolo.

Leticia Hernández-Linares

THE SPANGLISH SUPERHIGHWAY:
A ROAD MAP OF BICULTURAL SIGNS OF LIFE (2000-2003)

¡Propiedad Priba, Dano Traspasen!

On my wall, I have a photograph taken during a road trip along California Highway 101, somewhere near Salinas. My family and I came across a sign that read: "Propiedad Priba, Dano Traspasen," and we knew the sign meant to say "Private Property, Do not Trespass" in Spanish, but the letters not fitting all on one line, stuck together at the wrong places and transformed the phrase into something not quite Spanish, and not quite English. And yet, we recognized it.

My parents had emigrated from El Salvador eight years earlier and while we mainly spoke Spanish and English, Spanglish also eventually became part of our lingo. When we found the sign, it was the first public example we had seen outside of a Cheech and Chong movie, of words that violated both English and Spanish norms, as did we. For a while even my parents criticized and resisted this tongue twisting; we always lowered our voices to each other when we slipped into Spanglish. But as my father reached for the camera, that hesitance seemed to fall away as a historic picture taking moment for our family shed new light. Unlike language purists who might feel threatened by such grammatical liberties, we were super excitados by the sign's poetic license. We felt a strong connection to the sign, and we valued having proof of its existence—hence the Kodak moment and memento.

More and more, Spanglish has become recognized and has

begun shedding its image as a specter hovering over the allegedly pure languages of English and Spanish. When the government and media clumsily attempt to talk about Latin@s, however, because of their increasing numbers and subsequent importance as a voting base and market, the inability to break out of the mindset of "black or white" or "Spanish or English," still hinders an understanding of what are hybrid cultures. Spanglish has often been frowned upon for reasons that have motivated English-Only efforts—among them, the insistence on speaking *correctly*. Many Chican@s and Latin@s confront this problem by owning Spanglish, as well as Spanish, in order to show that assimilating into a homogenous monolingual culture is not the only way to succeed or to find a voice.

The latest wave of Spanglish speakers are taking control of the movement and hybridities that define us. It doesn't come in a neat package, however. And it doesn't involve an easily consumable culture that you can shake your hips and sing catchy lines to, so please, don't call it a "Latin explosion." This movida, this commotion, that has certainly been mounting since at least the 1970's when Chican@s began building a movement that confronted our struggles and fragmented identities, is gaining momentum—thanks to the work of artists, organizers, youth, and writers that are unapologetically expressing their complex identities publicly and crossing borders in the span of even just one sentence.

Englispan

For instance, in an After-School Spoken Word class that I taught in the Mission District of San Francisco in 2000, several of the middle school students experimented with writing freely (with no rules or corrections) and mixing the sounds of Spanish, English, and even Tagalog. Without thinking they couldn't, or for that matter shouldn't, they naturally switched from one language to another in a creative setting. One Latina student went so far as to make up her own word: "Englispan," to describe the third in her list of languages that she speaks:

> *My first languages are Spanish and English are three*
> Englispan
> I dream of flying[1]

The freedom to speak as they pleased helped build their confidence and fluency in whatever language challenged them, whether English or Spanish. On several occasions, they nervously, but bravely, publicly read poems referencing their families and ethnic identities.

Just in case, there's a nervous millionaire out there preparing a national campaign against Spanglish—relax Mr. Unz, let me clarify that no proposal for the replacement of either English or Spanish is being presented. Simply, the student's poetry represents what professor Ilán Stavans describes as an "inevitable country of immigrants." Author of *Spanglish: The Making of a New American Language*, Professor Stavans has taught classes such as "The Sounds of Spanglish" at Amherst College in Massachusetts. The first time he taught this course, in the Spanish Department no less, I spoke with Stavans, and, I seem to have consulted a Spanglish specialist. According to the brave Spanglish scholar, the "Sounds of Spanglish," explored Latino *culture* and the uniqueness of a population that speaks, whether it admits or realizes, in between two languages. History, linguistics, and art comprised some of the sources that Stavan's class drew on as it took a look at a way of speaking that not only very much exists, but might begin to answer the complex question: so who are these Latin@s and what do they want to be called exactly, *Hispanic, Spanish, Chicano*? What is most significant about this class and Stavan's book is the assertion in an academic context of the validity of Spanglish. This is what we speak, like it or not, and yes, we do not fit in the boxes.

Hech@s en Califas

This question of who we are is one Latin@ and Chican@ artists boldly explore throughout the country, as well as abroad. Let's go south for a minute to San Diego where a group of raza poets got together to present their words and music in taco shops. Ten years later, the Taco Shop Poets have traveled the country and appeared on television and film with the message that raza artists have their own multilingual expressions and have to create their own venues, and, they can. Speaking of community, a Chican@ family in San Diego, committed to self-determination created Calaca Press, and has since brought together intergenerational Chican@ voices with Central and South American ones. Chap-books, c.d.'s, poetry events, and most importantly, a network of artists are among the press' contributions to the movida de voces y identidades. Going back up North, an annual Latin@ arts festival *Hecho en Califas*, (made in California), has featured artists in various mediums who express their cultura on their terms. The festival focuses on showcasing the new wave of performers that reflect the contradictions within Latin@ identities.

But as we "read tacos, and eat poetry," as the introductory mantra to the Taco Shop Poets' website invites us to do, we are not offering you a *melting pot* of language, and it of course remains important for young people to become proficient in Spanish or English—moreover, those who make up the huge grouping "Latin@s," do not always know Spanish, let alone speak it. As the artists in this movement of Latin@ and Chican@ expression share their experiences, they do not generally pick out words as if they were at a flower shop, as embellishments. Rather, they present realities that are not completely translatable and audience friendly. In practice, Spanglish isn't as sexy as the "magically real" exoticism imposed on Spanish and its native speakers. When you unlock the gate and get past colorful skirts and smiling girls, you find broken Spanish, youth who favor Metallica, and Salvadoran immigrants who practice buddhism. It's a mix. In the past, there was a resistance and disdain of Spanglish and those who spoke it, which makes festivals like *Hecho en Califas* critical in representing cultural entities such as those "made" in Califas.

But as Paul Flores, creator and curator of the *Hecho* festivals points out, no "ready made audience," exists for artwork that reflects a bicultural experience and we see what happens—or rather it's what we don't see that is the problem—when mainstream media and venues portray Latin@s. The task that the young Latin@ and Chican@ generations face then is not simply to make Spanglish cultural expressions more public, but to continue creating the very spaces in which to present them.

Once such venue, Espresso Mi Cultura in Hollywood, is a café, bookstore, art gallery, and community center all in one, and represents what co-owner Josie Aguilar explains as the "unyielding fatih in our [Latin@s'] ability to empower ourselves on all fronts." Many businesses such as this one have begun to open in Los Angeles and San Diego, and like Aguilar, these entrepreneurs are establishing their spaces in neighborhoods that need economic revitalization. Espresso Mi Cultura, comprehensive in everything from its name, to its merchandise, to its events, provides a model suggesting that through a cultural and practical focus, organizing might be possible for such a fragmented group.

La Cucaracha has to Walk the Walk

As many of the haz lo tu mismo…do-it-yourself trends are trying to show, it's not enough to suggest that well, this is how we speak, "¡¿y qué?!" As political satirist and columnist Lalo Lopez Alcaraz emphasized to me in our dialogue about the Spanglish buzz "its really what you are saying, not what language you say it in." This insight about the importance to educate and inform distinguishes Alcaraz's long history of Spanglish trailblazing through his comic strip and multimedia productions from say Schwarzenegger's infamous bilingual good-bye or Ricky's crazy life. As one of the most unapologetic Spangliphiles around, Alcaraz began writing the Spanglish script way before it was popular. Having begun with *Pocho Magazine* in the early 90's, he still employs Spanglish in his political commentary and cartoon strip "La Cucaracha." One of my many favorites in his now syndicated column is La Pochahontas, the princess wearing layers of aqua net that you need to watch out for—and wáchala with that Americanized girl from the barrio, because she don't play.

Spanglish even seems to be emerging as a global phenomenon, which explains why Stavans teaches his class in Spanish and looks at Spanglish in Latin America as well. For a long time associated just with Chican@ culture, Spanglish has shown to have an impact in different Latin American countries. Writer Mario Bencastro in his chapbook *Vato Guanaco Loco: Rap en caliche* (The Crazy Salvadoran Dude: Rap in Salvadoran slang), takes a look at the linguistic mixtures and revisions that have made their way to El Salvador. Terms such as "yunaites" (as in the Yunaites States) are among the Spanglish soundbites that fall in line next to the arrival of the almighty dollar, the mass deportation of gang members from Los Angeles, and the high volume of travel by struggling immigrants and would-be commuters. In 2000, I found myself somewhere between the immigrants and commuters, as I joined a delegation of Salvadoran artists and organizers to El Salvador. We swallowed our pride, and put our Spanglish tendencies out on the table for all the "authentic" Salvadorans to see. We gathered at La Luna Casa de Arte, an arthouse in San Salvador, for a conference, Foro 2000, a presentation of performance, poetry, visual art, film, and literary analysis. Throughout our travels, we visited archives dedicated to preserving the records of Salvadoran literary and social history as we spent time explaining how we uniquely and bilingually fit into that history. In the years since, a Central American Poetry group, Epicentro has emerged and, throughout California, pushed generations of Salvadoran and Central American immigrants and their children onto the radar of the U.S. Latin@ literary scene. This is an important moment for Central Americans in the U.S. as we express how we aren't Salvadoran or Honduran or Chicano, but something in between, and at the same time, all those of things. Gaps within the gaps. Púchica, vos, it never ends.

Split Tongues

The gaps persist, however, and a reluctance to recognize and validate the symbols of biculturalism continues especially on the Northern side of the U.S. Mexico border. Thus, Spanglish becomes a symbol of resistance on cultural terms, that challenges the dated assimilation model of success. It just is no longer as simple as you are either assimilated or newly immigrated; even some new immigrants arrive already affected by mainstream North American culture and the English language, and furthermore, not all of us are immigrants. On both sides of the border, we need to appreciate the validity of the culture that exists between the Latin Americans and "Americans." Specifically regarding Latin@s, while it is important to elucidate the problems with the way the terms "Hispanic" and "Latino" lump and homogenize people with important differences, it doesn't suffice it to conclude that the term "Hispanic" just does not work, since it is not a "race"—as if the concept of "different races" itself is somehow valid in any context. Moreover, in light of such simplistic arguments, the racism against Latin@s is overlooked. The complexities of how Latin@s have been constructed—marginalized, racialized, commodified—will require many translators and new forums, for sure.

The various "it's either one or the other" camps nervously watch this battle of the languages—really nationalism in disguise—fighting to hold on as biculturalism pushes at too many boundaries. On a national level, the linguistic playing fields remain very much in flux for Latin@ groups. In the last few years, twenty-two states have gone the extra mile to declare English their official language, a movement led by Chilean born Mauro Mujica. Mujica is the proud Chairman and CEO of U.S. ENGLISH Inc., a "citizen action group" concerned with privileging the English language. Thanks to this company, several states have passed official English measures, a merely symbolic, but nonetheless, powerful manifestation of the need to assert the superiority of one language and one culture. The worry expressed on both sides of the language border reminds me of that priceless scene in the film *Born in East L.A.* when border crossers stampede towards some very scared border patrol guards and Neil Diamond belts out "Coming to America" in the background. I wonder, when my grandmother who speaks about a word for every year she has lived and worked in the U.S., talks about the day she became an "American City" does her mispronunciation conjure images of stampedes of words across language frontiers?

Yes, even my grandmother speaks Spanglish, senk yoom

very much. Thinking on her interesting mispronunciations, I wonder about the future North American city and what it will not only look, but sound like. I suspect that English and Spanish will continue evolving as the hybrid languages that they already are, and I expect that cultural borders will become more fluid not in order to obscure or melt down many cultures into one, but rather to connect and clarify them to each other.

In English "to enter private property without authorization" is the definition for the word "trespass." The Spanish word "traspasar" means to pierce like a bullet or soak through liquid. Appropriately, we need to pierce through the idea of U.S. Latin@s as a group that has trespassed in language or presence into the U.S. I mean, who is trespassing...ay, but that is another road trip, one we've taken before...

Anyway, so I leave you, with un saludo from una chica Salvi-Latina-Chicana-Guanaca-speaking not being Spanish-not Hispanic-pero poetisa-singing bits of Nahuatl and Yoruba-born in Nuestra Señora de Los Angeles de Porciuncula-living in San Pancho-but conceived between tropics and volcanoes, from black sand. And *that*, is *just* the beginning.

Bueno pues, ay los wach-o. All right then, I'll see you later. Will you see me?

---

1) Victoria Jimenez, *Forever Words Beyond: Writings by Horace Mann Middle School Students*, Jamestown Community Center, 2000.

Celeste Guzman Mendoza

NATIVE TONGUE

"So, you don't speak your native tongue, do you?"

The comment dropped out of the mouth of Professor X and one of my…eek!…advisors during my freshman year at my Ivy League alma mater.

I was standing by the copier, copying away the last hour of one of my three work-study jobs.

After asking if I spoke Spanish "fluently" and me responding, "Well, a mix of Spanish and English—Tex-Mex, you know" he blurted out the "native tongue" comment that he then continued to repeat like a mantra throughout our conversation while I tried to hurry the old copier through its staple, sort, double-sided job of 200 copies.

The copier groaned and creaked and I wanted to scream, "I feel your pain!" because I felt the, here-is-another-academic-explaining-my-ethnic-reality feeling coming on.

Professor X supposedly was a genius, not a social one obviously. He famed himself on being able to answer any question with a pretty elaborate response that routinely included at least ten words of more than four syllables and that contained approximately 3.5 compound sentences—in English only. He was Jewish, from the Bronx, proud he was Jewish from the Bronx, had a beard, rounded glasses a-la-John-Lennon and loved brown sweaters and beige slacks.

He was Jewish and spoke no Yiddish or Hebrew so when he let drop the "native tongue" question, despite his sarcastic tone, I initially thought we were going to find a point of connection. We both obviously respected our ethnic traditions—I was wearing a rebozo while I made my copies and he kept his beard long. I thought we were going to both talk about how our parents went through so much prejudice because they were more fluent in another language than English, how they weren't served in some places when they spoke that language, how when they were young they had to pay 25 cents each time they said a word in their "native tongue", how every time they watched TV somebody was making fun of the way they talked English, or worse when they took the bus or went for a walk downtown they were called names for not being mainstream Anglo-American and speaking accent-free English, "Speak English! English!"

But, I was wrong.

He let the candor fall freely, "Oh, so you have no culture then. Aseemoolaudau."

The copier jammed.

After unjamming the copier by following its beeps and flashes, I started in on my explain-to-academic-my-ethnic-reality speech. That Mexican-Americans from Texas came from various cultures and that some of us spoke Spanish, English, Tex-Mex, and many other languages. I explained that my grandparents and parents were fined money, regarded as idiots, and slapped daily by a ruler on the knuckles solely because they could conjugate verbs in Spanish better than in English and that in order for me to not experience that type of discrimination my parents had made sure that I knew my English well, as they both had worked extra hard to know it well. I told him that I was majoring in English and that my parents were proud of my entering an Ivy League school in New York where they were sure that I wouldn't have to deal with discrimination like I may have experienced in Texas.

He didn't get it.

He went on to say how "sad" he was for me. That I had "lost my culture." That I was "not really Lauteenau."

At that point, I picked up all 200 unsorted and unstapled copies and left Professor X alone with the old, groaning copier.

Unfortunately, there was his class the next day. He was an advisor for a special research project I was awarded. The next day in class when he noticed that my name on my paper did not have an accent, the accent that I had never nor my grandparents or parents had ever put on our last name, he flicked the paper at me while slipping in, "Aseemoolaudau," in front of the entire class. Of course, we were the only two that understood exactly what the word meant. Nobody else in the class was bilingual—Spanish or any other language. But I think even they got his general message.

The next afternoon I was in the Dean's office telling her what Professor X had let drop at the copier and slip the day before. She was shocked as Professor X was one of their "finest" professors and was on the college's Diversity Committee, she told me, and he himself, like her, was Jewish. He should understand. She did.

After listening to me for about half an hour explain in English about my father serving in Vietnam, my grandfather fleeing Mexico, my other grandfather traveling all over the country to pick cotton, ALL in the name of the United States and English—oh, and by the way, I paid to go to college I deserved better—she said that I was right, I did deserve better. She would make sure the incidents would be documented in Professor X's personnel file and, in plain English, he would need to apologize to me.

The next class he asked me outside for a private conversation. He asked me why I went to the Dean when I could have spoken with him directly. Why I had to go over his head for something that was not such a big deal and that I took his comments wrong. I really didn't have any culture—how could I if I didn't speak my "native tongue?" Didn't I understand he was helping me, helping me regain who I was, who I had lost because I had no "native tongue." I should be thankful that he was taking such an interest in empowering his female students of color.

The genius couldn't get it. He also couldn't apologize.

Ironically, later in the semester Professor X told the class that although he was Jewish he didn't speak Yiddish or Hebrew. Couldn't understand a word. He said that his father was furious at him for it, that his father felt he was less Jewish because he couldn't converse in Hebrew or Yiddish like a proper Jewish man. Professor X said that he disagreed with his father. He felt that he didn't have to know Yiddish or Hebrew to be Jewish. That being Jewish was a state of mind and daily practice.

I am not sure why my Latinaness was not also a state of mind and daily practice. Why for him my Latinaness, my authenticity as a Latina, was measured by my use or non-use of my "native tongue", which he automatically assumed was Spanish as opposed to Catalán or Nahuatl or English.

Three years after the copier incident, the college made a video about Latinas on campus—our life in the classroom, at home, and our family. It would be viewed by all the professors that worked at the college and then would be distributed to other Ivy League sister schools so that those professors too could understand their Latina students better. So that other professors would not repeat the "native tongue" mantra or perhaps to protect the schools from court appearances.

I am not crazy enough to think that my single experience or my single complaint to the Dean caused the video to be created but I am sure that if I had stayed quiet nothing would have been done to educate Professor X about how offensive and disrespect-ful the "native tongue" comment was and about how extremely uneducated he was about the U.S. Latino language experience.

In the video, I told this same story knowing that he would see it. Knowing that other professors like him would see it. Knowing that they too had said it—perhaps—or thought it.

I knew he would be on the Committee that would make the edits to the video, that would decide what would stay and what wouldn't. But I also knew that the Dean too would be there.

When I saw the final cut, it was there. Me, sitting in a chair, a lamp on a small side table, my rebozo wrapped loosely on my shoulders. I hadn't remembered looking into the camera and say-ing, my eyes intent, "My Latinaness will not be defined by you. It is mine. You cannot have it. You are not an expert. I am. I live it."

No, we have no right to categorize what is lived. Language, identity—they don't inhabit a single category. They exist and like all organisms they transform, adapt, and adopt to survive—never loosing but amending, not always making amends, but surviving nonetheless.

Stephanie Li

THE SECRET AMERICAN

I avoid looking at myself in mirrors, my reflection a reminder that I don't really know what I look like. The face in the mirror surprises me, never quite what I expected though I am not sure what that would be. I puzzle over my features. Is my profile so flat? Has my nose changed shape somehow? And those eyebrows, so heavy and dark, who do they belong to? I don't look like anyone I know. In family pictures, I tower over my parents, nothing but my arms stretched behind their shoulders to suggest that we are related. Somehow I grew to be more than six feet tall even though my mother shops in the petite section of department stores, and my father keeps a footstool handy in the kitchen. They joke that my height is the result of having been fed so well as a child, a good, healthy American diet. My hair is long and straight, my mother's short and curly. And though I have looked, I have nothing of her patient, steady gaze. People say my eyes change color—brown, green, whatever hazel looks like—while hers match my father's chocolate eyes. Usually I am just a shade lighter than his toasted complexion, but after a long winter I can become as pale as my mother though never with her rosy hue.

We look like strangers to one another, our faces perfectly distinct, especially in the suburbs of Kansas City where they now live, a place, my mother says, where everyone looks like they are related to each other. Even my mother's family cannot pretend that there's much of a resemblance between me and any of my army of cousins. You'd think with so many people—all the primos and the ones who aren't really primos but still considered blood, though only I would notice the difference—at least one of them would resemble me. Instead I am the gringa that doesn't look like one, dark hair and glasses where there should be blonde ringlets and blue eyes.

Strangers and new acquaintances inevitably ask me where I am from. Usually I make them guess, and while they purse their eyebrows and bite their lips, I try to predict their answers. The businessman with the red face and soft white hair will think I was born in Korea, but was adopted as an infant by a nice, well-to-do family since of course I speak perfectly, no trace of an accent. A woman with a Southern drawl will point her index finger at me, and proclaim, "Indian for sure though who knows what tribe." She'll touch her chin, adding, "And some white blood I suppose." With one hand on my shoulder, she'll laugh and say, "But isn't that all of us, honey?" I've been mistaken for everything from black to white. Outside of the United States, I am typically assumed to be some type of Asian—Japanese, Polynesian perhaps—never American. But here, in my country, I can be anything.

I am never quite sure what people see when they look at me. We study each other carefully, casting speculations, waiting for some clue to slip out. With polite scrutiny, they assess my cheek-bones, the color of my skin, listen for the hint of an accent and puzzle at my height, while I smile and nod, trying to gauge what it is they see. When the guessing game is over, I usually reply by saying that I was born in the Midwest, but my family moved around while I was growing up. After a few years teaching at a public high school, I now attend graduate school in upstate New York. I offer these details with the hope of shifting the conversation elsewhere—the Midwest climate, the sorry state of public education, teenagers these days, my graduate work in American literature—something real and definable.

Instead I hear, "Sure, but where are you really from?"

The only answer that makes sense is "When?"

When I first moved to New York three years ago, I was from California where I attended college and worked for a few years after graduation. When I started college I was from Kansas City even though I had only lived there a year, and had spent the first three years of high school in a small town in Washington State. But of course the truth is that I was really born in Minneapolis, a city I don't care to remember. None of this is what they want to hear, nor is it anything I want to be reminded of, so at last I say, "My father is Chinese, my mother is Mexican," hoping they don't catch the edge of defeat in my voice. Looking past the sudden delight of their discovery, I nod and raise my eyebrows as if to share in their surprise. Yes, it's quite an unusual combination. A rich heritage of course. Yes, in fact both of my parents are excellent cooks.

It's of no concern that my father's family has lived and worked in the United States for generations and to call him "Chinese" is a false shorthand, that since 1986 my mother has been a U.S. citizen, and that the only language spoken in my house is English.

When I was a child I used to recite to adults, "I'm half Chinese, half Mexican, but all American." I'm not sure how I developed this diversity cheer, but by the time I started elementary school, I couldn't rely on that cute slogan to help me understand my obvious, but slippery difference from all the other kids in my class. No one identifies herself as white when everyone is, just like no one speaks of ethnicity, race, or nationality when everyone belongs.

Even though we spoke the same adolescent slang, pledged allegiance to the same flag, and the color of my skin was sometimes no different than that of my peers, we were not the same.

When friends came over to my house after school, they asked about the chopsticks in the kitchen drawers, holding them out like batons or swords, and they wanted to know why my mother spoke funny. Even now I have trouble hearing her accent. Of course I know she doesn't speak like everyone else, but she doesn't speak different. Except perhaps when she's very tired, and she'll call me "Estephanie" before drifting off to sleep.

In fifth grade I started taking Spanish and like all the other kids in my class, I didn't speak a word past "taco" and "nachos." A group of girls named themselves after their cleaning ladies, Rosa, Elena, and Dolores. I giggled along with them even though my family didn't have a cleaning lady, and one of my favorite tías is named Rosa. But no one knew that, and no one would.

After only a few weeks of class, I discovered that I knew much more Spanish than my classmates, but when asked, I attributed my mysterious knowledge to extra hours studying, not to annual trips to my grandmother's house in Monterrey or the memory of bedtime lullabyes. I sometimes told my friends that I was spending my spring break in Cancun rather than in my mother's land-locked, industrial hometown, reasoning that to them it was all just Mexico, someplace far away, warm, and poor. When I returned, no one ever asked me why I didn't have a tan.

Although my mother started teaching my older brother to speak Spanish when he was a child, by the time I was born that arrangement had ended. My brother couldn't have been more than four years old when one afternoon he told her that he thought they should stop speaking Spanish together since "Daddy didn't understand." And with that they stopped.

I was well into high school before I realized the loss it was not to have been raised bilingual. By then my tongue had hard-ened around the sounds of American English, and I was unable to mimic the smooth cadence of a native Spanish speaker. I have never been able to roll my r's and despite my best efforts, my textbook Spanish is still laced with an American twang. On visits to my family in Monterrey, there is always an awkward moment of hesitation when I first see my relatives – to speak to me in English or Spanish? Either one is somehow a mistake.

I once told my mother that she should have taught us to speak Spanish. That the benefits of being bilingual far outweighed my brother's original concerns. I talked about it as an academic advantage, a career asset, a useful life skill, but I was thinking of how much easier it would have made our visits to Monterrey. How the hours sitting around my grandmother's kitchen table wondering what everyone was saying, trying to glean meaning from facial expressions and changes in tone might have been transformed into something comprehensible, familiar. Did it really bother my father that he didn't understand Spanish? I continued as my mother listened to my unexpected harangue. She had been trimming her favorite ivy, but now she sat quiet, her hands folded on the kitchen table.

It was my brother who had assumed that Spanish was a problem. Maybe Dad would have preferred that we speak it. Did she ever ask him? And shouldn't her husband know her native language anyway? Why didn't he speak Spanish too? How could she have followed the advice of a child so easily? She sat patiently through the whole of my rant, nodding at times as she smoothed out the folds of the kitchen tablecloth, watching my cheeks flush without saying a word. And when I stopped, there was a long pause of silence, as if she was waiting in case I needed to say more. Her courtesy was deafening.

Maybe you're right, she murmured. It's just that we were so alone. We had to be strong, united. I didn't want to risk that.

There was nothing more to say. I knew exactly what she was talking about. The four of us living first in Minnesota and then in Washington were a tiny island, adrift in a huge sea. There were no grandparents, uncles, or aunts within reach, no cousins to play with after school or old family friends to call for a weekend visit or a dinner at a favorite restaurant. Neither were there church groups or neighborhood organizations, no community at all.

When my parents decided to put up a fence on the one side of our backyard that was not already enclosed, the woman next door complained that it was a return to the Alamo. My father said, no, the Great Wall, and although I did not understand what he meant, when I forgot my house key a few weeks later, I took a long walk through the neighborhood until my brother came home from soccer practice. Though it was never explicitly mentioned, I knew that part of my difference from the kids I met at school or on the playground was that unlike their families, mine was all alone.

Of course people were friendly to us. My grade school teachers were delighted to have my parents help out in the classroom. On Christmas we received bins of popcorn and fruit baskets from my parents' co-workers. But always there was a distance. When guests came over for dinner, they called the brush paintings and wall hangings in the living room "exotic," and even when my father had only cooked a simple meal, the food was always "unusual." When our guests waved good bye and returned to their own suburban homes, I breathed a sigh of relief. With the door closed against the winter winds and the kind strangers who despite their best, most sincere intentions would always be strangers, I relaxed back into the comfort of our small but safe home.

The four of us—my father, mother, brother, and me—made up a tight if narrow safety net. We always ate dinner together, spent weekends at museums and parks, and in the evenings my mother checked my homework before we all gathered to play card games or watch a favorite television program. I realize now that the type of unity that existed in my family is rare in most American households, and I was shocked to learn that some of my friends never ate with their parents, or received help on school projects. And then it seems that of course we had to speak only one language between us. We were all we had.

Even if my mother had tried to teach me Spanish during my childhood, I am not sure that I would have consented to the lessons. I wanted desperately to belong, to have a grandmother who made apple pie and chocolate chip cookies, to look like the girls at school with their light hair and round blue eyes. Spanish would have been another secret, a language only for the home, a home which was already too small.

A few years ago my mother told me that when my brother and I were children, she was afraid of angering us too much. She scolded and punished us when we fought or failed to complete our chores, but she said that she was always careful to give us the space to return to her. "What else could you do? Who could you have gone to?" she asked and the silence that followed frightened me.

My mother was raised in a family of seven. When tempers flared there was always someone else to turn to, an empathetic tía or cousin who listened, made sense of ugly words and hurt feelings, someone who could always turn tears into laughter. But if something broke between the four of us, there would be nothing left.

We learned to be careful with one another. When my mother told me stories of our relatives in Mexico I wondered at their audacity, their passion and vehemence. Mothers yell at daughters, daughters yell back and their sisters and brothers take sides, insulting one another with awful precision or maybe just laughing as they go on with their own overstuffed lives.

I've seen them. They laugh more, cry harder, they indulge every emotion that strikes them. When we visit, I sit on my hands and smile when I don't know what else to do. Like when Lolita whispers to me that our tía Josefina still eats supper across a framed picture of her husband even though he has been dead for seven years. I don't know whether to laugh or nod solemnly. Is Lolita only teasing me? Testing how much a gringa will believe? She shrugs it off with a smile and tells me that one of my younger cousins has bruises on his knees from falling on the floor in his frequent battles with Satan.

I am glad that no one asks what my life is like. It is either so alien to them as to be beyond description, or more likely, it simply doesn't exist for them. They have lives like soap operas while here we are something else, more prudent perhaps. Yes, and more rational, my father might say, not so excessive. We are careful and careful to be careful. Rage and fury are words I learned in books. My parents taught my brother and I to reason out our disagreements, to discuss conflicts in order to reach a fair and workable compromise. We don't yell, or threaten to never speak to one another again. This is not just care and prudence, this is survival.

When I go to Mexico I am always the outsider looking in. I listen to their stories and it's like listening to what happened at a party that I always miss. If someone forgot to invite me, it certainly wasn't on purpose or maybe it was me who made an excuse and decided not to come. There's no going back, my father said when he returned from his first and only visit to China. He had gone on business but also to see if maybe there would be something, some connection to the people, to the culture. A feeling perhaps of belonging, of return. Instead he came back to Kansas City and announced, "You know I'm not really Chinese."

I pointed out that he didn't want to be Chinese, he never bothered to learn Mandarin, never sought out a Chinese community, doesn't even follow the political situation in China. He nodded. "I suppose you're right," he said, "it's just that no one besides us knows that."

"You're a secret American," I said, and we laughed because we had no one to tell our secrets to.

Carlos C. Amaya

EL NACIMIENTO

Los caminos se cruzaban para seguir hacia la ermita o la escuela, respectivamente. Tantas veces habían pasado por allí sin nunca haber imaginado lo que podría suceder cualquier día. La tarde había caído y empezaban a verse las luciérnagas y los tras-traces encender sus lucecitas. Habían caminado como hora y media y se acercaban a la encrucijada que los llevaría a su morada. De repente, entre las tinieblas de la tarde, se vio una sombra que desapareció delante de ellos en la curva próxima que se extendía a unos varios pasos. No había sido una visión muy clara pero si certera, se había visto que las hojas se movieron como si una corriente de aire se las llevara y luego silencio y quietud nada más. Las sombras del crepúsculo siempre le habían parecido espantosas por lo del folklore local que contaba sobre aparecidos y espíritus malignos. Aquella instantánea visión había caído más pesada sobre su joven imaginación. En su cabeza resonaban las historias del pericón, del Cipitillo y la Siguanaba que tantas veces les había relatado su abuelita en la casa de la finca. Aunque su cuerpo temblaba de punta a punta y sus ojos se turbaban del miedo por la oscuridad, lo cual era incrementado por la densa vegetación del lugar, cubierto de grandes guarumos, hojas blancas, bambúes y otros árboles de densa vegetación de las que abundan en el trópico, seguía mirando atentamente hacia las profundidades del monte con un valor inexplicable en aquellas circunstancias.

En el fondo de su cabeza aparecía una imagen que él creía haber visto por una milésima de segundo. Al llegar al cruce su padre comenzó a correr de repente con la pistola en una mano y el mache en la otra. Le gritaba como loco que cargara el fusil y le disparara a la sombra que corría enfrente de ellos tratando de escaparse y lanzando unos terribles aullidos. Esos pocos pero interminables segundos le parecieron una vida. Casi por instinto y sin pensar en lo que decía él también comenzó a gritar. ¡No! ¡No es él! ¡Espérese! Cada grito retumbaba con ecos macabros en las copas de los árboles que formaban una bóveda como la de una catedral. No sé cuántas veces gritó y cuántas veces se escucharon sus alaridos de súplica por aquellas fincas que se extendían por kilómetros a la redonda. El ¡NO! seguía resonando por las cortezas, las raíces, las hojas y las flores de los árboles y hasta por las piedras del camino que rodaban pendiente abajo.

¿Qué pasaría si hacía lo que su padre le pedía y que pasaría si no lo hacía? ¿Qué tal si él tenía razón y era el zarco? ¿Los mataría? ¿Los haría pedazos y les sacaría los ojos como había hecho con los guardias aquellos que muchos años antes lo habían tratado de capturar? La historia la había escuchado muchas veces y sabía bien lo que podría pasarles en aquel lugar desolado y oscuro aquella tarde de invierno. Pero, dudaba. Dudaba porque en el fondo sabía que no era el zarco. La imagen se le repetía en la cabeza. Sabía que había visto un sombrero de tule manchado por la tierra y el sudor de su dueño. No era felpa ni mucho menos pelo. Estaba seguro que lo había visto. De repente dio un gran salto. Un rayo lo había sacado de su interminable debate interior. Por unos instantes había perdido contacto con la realidad. Un segundo rayo y otro y otro. En su congoja y tembladera del cuerpo se dio cuenta que no eran rayos, eran balazos que retumbaban en el castillo negro que formaban las copas de los árboles.

Gritó con todas sus fuerzas al punto que sintió que se le reventaban los pulmones. Gritó otra vez antes que resonara el siguiente estallido. Siguió gritando para que no siguiera disparando a la vez que su padre gritaba que disparara con el potente rifle de caza. En ese intercambio logró articular que era don Rosendo el que acababa de pasar. Por obra y gracia del creador y gracias a la oscuridad que dominaba el lugar, su padre había fallado. Los gritos de terror del hombre que corría como alma que llevaba el diablo se escuchaban aun hasta cuando había desaparecido en la distancia penumbrosa del lugar. Cuando todo acabó, cayó hincado de terror de pensar sobre la desgracia que podía haber ocurrido. Pero en su cabeza estaba convencido que si hubiera sido el zarco no lo habría dudado, le habría disparado.

Margarita Pignataro

A FIFTEEN MINUTE INTERVIEW WITH A LATINA

This play was written and performed for the Underrepresented Graduate Scholars event, Portraits of the Latina/o Identity, that took place at State University of New York at Stony Brook on October 29, 1999.

CHARACTERS
INTERVIEWER: A female Indian psychiatrist in a sari.
INTERVIEWEE: A disturbed Latina dressed with a gypsy skirt, alpaca Chilean looking sweater, underneath a torn, soiled, T-shirt with the word Chile across the front, and a colorful handkerchief covering her hair.

SETTING: Doctor's office. Two chairs with a small round table in between and a tall floor plant. A white strait jacket in the corner.

INTERVIEWER seated in a chair with pen in hand, clip board and folder on lap. Enter slowly stage right INTERVIEWEE.

INTERVIEWER: Ay, take a seat please. (Points to chair directly in front of her.) I see here your name is (looks at the paper in her folder.) Marialita Balseos Pignatorio. Um...is that a Cuban name? (More to herself than INTERVIEWER.) Marialita Balseos. I can't seem to pronounce it. (Tries to pronounce it again.)

INTERVIEWEE: (Passive.) No. It's pronounced...

INTERVIEWER: You must be from Florida correct?

(INTERVIEWEE throughout the interview is shifting in her seat.)

INTERVIEWEE: (Surprised.) Florida? (To herself.) Cuba? My only relationship with Cuba is my godfather who was part of the 60's wave. Ay, espérate. (To INTERVIEWER.) I believe you may have my name confused with los marielitos and los balseros. Ja ja my name is pronounced...

INTERVIEWER: (Clears throat.) I wanted to ask some questions related to your background and experience here in the United States. Which will bring us to the state you are in right now.

INTERVIEWEE: That's why I'm here because I understand everywhere.

INTERVIEWER: Yes, mmm, now tell me (takes paper out of folder). You are 35 years old and fluent in Spanish and you were born here so my first question is, (pause) how is it that you have become fluent in the language and many Hispanics have not?

INTERVIEWEE: Well, um...

INTERVIEWER: Take your time.

INTERVIEWEE: I spoke it with my family members and hung out with ecuatorianos in the neighborhood. After learning the different home idioms and dialects I was placed in an institution where they engraved rules and a standard way of speaking Spanish.

INTERVIEWER: Oh, I see. So the Hispanics who don't speak Spanish really haven't put forth the effort that is involved with speaking the language, correct?

INTERVIEWEE: Well, the logic is if you don't use it you lose it, but those Hispanics who don't speak Spanish may have been in a different environment.

INTERVIEWER: For example?

INTERVIEWEE: For example, a Hispanic around non-Spanish speaking people or Hispanics around Hispanics that don't talk fluent or conversational Spanish.

INTERVIEWER: Like the Chicagos in California.

INTERVIEWEE: That would be Chicanos and they are not only in California or the Southwest, but all over the States. They've been in the U.S. for so many generations that modern Spanish is their creation. I think the Chicanos are the first generation Spanglish speakers, or hybrid creators, or some term like that. Don't get me wrong. Their traditional customs are alive, but as far as language, it's one thing to know words and sayings and another to know the standard.

INTERVIEWER: Standard? That's the second time you mention the word. Could you elaborate on (makes quotation marks with fingers) "standard" please?

INTERVIEWEE: Well, it's not slang and it's not a dialect. It's a straight-forward type of Spanish. Normal you may say, proper would be another adjective. Standard places you in the category of an educated native speaker.

INTERVIEWER: You plan an escape to a Native Spanish speaking country to find if it is true, do you?

INTERVIEWEE: Yea, my heart aches. All these varieties in the U.S.A. ay, it forces me to focus on my Latin American roots.

INTERVIEWER: Yes, I understand, but how about the proper way of speaking?

INTERVIEWEE: Well, it's great if you are in an academic environment, and I'll continue to check it out in the South. I remember I was confused when I first started standard and now, at times, I get frustrated. Ay! Then I just find it plain boring.

INTERVIEWER: Umm, please go on. Elaborate on why the confusion. Feel free to express the different feelings on each dialect you have experienced.

INTERVIEWEE: Excuse me?

INTERVIEWER: I am saying to explain to me in your own creative way the feelings you have when you encountered Spanish at a young age and when you entered the institution. Could you relate to each dialect now?

INTERVIEWEE: Sure, I haven't forgotten anything. In fact I have rebelled.

INTERVIEWER: In what way have you rebelled?

INTERVIEWEE: Well, I try to use as little as possible of the standard when I'm out of the complex. You see, if I'm too standard then street won't understand and I forget how to relate with family. I feel weird, but in a backward sense.

INTERVIEWER: I don't think I quite understand.

INTERVIEWEE: Think of it like this: for years what you thought was ¿Cómo estái? was actually ¿Cómo estás? And ¿Qué hora son? in standard is ¿Qué hora es? Now, even though I know the standard, I revert to ¿Cómo estái? and ¿Qué hora son? around my family because I don't want to feel like an outsider. I know hora is singular and that is why you say qué hora es, however, my family knows the response will be "son las" whatever number and uses ¿Qué hora son? Call it misinterpreting the rules, but I know what my family has said and now I know that trabajai and estudiái are not standard words. (More to herself.) I wonder about the standards in the Andes.

INTERVIEWER: (Very interested and eager. Go on about the standard and institution.

INTERVIEWEE: (Shifting in the chair.) More? What else can I share? I felt comfortable with Spanish, got into the institution and felt weird. My ¿Oye huevona cómo estái? Suddenly changed to ¿Cómo está usted? Then I got out of the institution and instead of feeling comfortable because I knew the standard I felt displaced! I can't explain to you in English my experience of the different Spanish dialects. I have to demonstrate what I experienced in

Spanish.

INTERVIEWER: Well, don't get nervous. Remember to breathe deep breaths, diaphragmatic breaths. (Demonstrates.) Now you try.

INTERVIEWEE (Breathes.)

INTERVIEWER: Now, continue with the breathing and share with me your Spanish experience.

INTERVIEWEE: Well, it all started...do you think I can move around? It's just that I don't do well still.

INTERVIEWER: Too passionate (nods head) I understand. Yes, (hand gestures) do stand up, dance, do what you must and start with your childhood.

INTERVIEWEE: Thank you. Well, I've always been in an environment of diverse Spanish speakers. At age six, I would hear my godfather say things like: ¿Cómo ehtah? Cuando ehtaba en Cuba, tu papá y yo terminabamos en el conuco con una copita de ron. I also remember hearing from my parent's Puerto Rican friends: Nena! ¿Cómo tú ehtah? Embustera, tú pai no viene pol qué no arranca el cajo. Ven a casa a comel. I mean I've heard deep-rooted accents true communication with flavor. (Stares out to the audience.)

INTERVIEWER: Go on. Any... (gestures with her hands) other groups?

INTERVIEWEE: En la Florida, México y Arizona I interacted with los mexicanos. Ándale pues. Órale pues. ¿Cómo estás herma-naaaaa? And los argentinos, che Magui ese pibre siempre anda con el porro. The funny thing is that I don't know how to speak Spanish even though I comprehend all these dialects and have gone to the Spanish speaking countries. (Meditative.) I still am not owner of my accent.

INTERVIEWER: What do you mean your accent?

INTERVIEWEE: Well, I'm chilena and I move into and out of specific Latino groups hearing all the dialects and intonations. The Chilean accent doesn't come natural to me because I have lived in other communities. My accent is the American accent with a twist of all the various Spanish dialects. One minute and you get this: (Argentinean accent) Che Magui, ¿vas a conducir en esta lluvia? (Chilean accent) ¿Qué estái loca? Además no quiero que salgái con ese tipo poh. (Puerto Rican accent) Pol que chacha tú tieneh que tenel cuidao con ehtoh que no tienen chavoh. (Mexican accent) Ese chico te vigila porque pues necesita una chavala para conseguir la visa. (Cuban accent) Margaritica no no no no por nada mi cielito ese no te conviene. Or something like that.

INTERVIEWER: You did that very well. You do have the advantage to know a very diverse language and be connected to so many people.

INTERVIEWEE: Sí, now I think that I need a break from me, from American me, from the Spanish that sounds like a rock scraping the inner ears of all natives Spanish speakers. With the strength of my ancestor's ancestors, I will go to my forefather's country and learn who I am. I can not conform to the Latina status. I refuse the consumption of material objects. The focus must be to develop my voice in society. I need to know what that voice says. I need Chile.

INTERVIEWER: And how will you accomplish that?

INTERVIEWEE: I shall voyage to Chile to observe the reflection I should have mirrored all the years people thought of me from Chile and not from the United States.

INTERVIEWER: You lied? You said you were from Chile and not the United States?

INTERVIEWEE: No. (Whining.) I didn't lie. They just didn't believe me! Where are you from? they would ask. Massachusetts, I would reply. They would laugh (fake laugh) ja, and then say, no come on, where are you really from? Or sometimes they would say, no, you know what I mean. After I told them Chile they would say, that's what I thought, that's what I wanted, or some messed up comment así.

INTERVIEWER: People didn't believe you from the U.S. so you had to say you where from Chile for them to accept you?

INTERVIEWEE: I guess. I was Puerto Rican, Mexican or Cuban and any other group placed me into a special category. ¿Qué sé yo?

INTERVIEWER: One more question and then you can rest a bit.

INTERVIEWEE: Oh, at night, do I still have to wear that white suit to sleep again? The color is okay, it just gets uncomfortable at times.

INTERVIEWER: After we'll talk about that. One more thing I wondered. The last name how did that happen?

INTERVIEWEE: Well, I think the story went something like this. My grandfather was Italian from Calabria and he came to the United States in his thirties. He didn't have a license, no transportation and basically he was illegal. Well, he met my grandmother who was Chilean, Sicilian, and born in the Untied States. He was so amazed that he could run into an Italian who was born in the States, that to make sure he wasn't wasting time with a non citizen, he asked my grandmother 6 times on the first date if she was born in the States.

INTERVIEWER: Six times?

INTERVIEWEE: Yea, six times. You know why don't you?

INTERVIEWER: For the things he didn't have being an illegal I suppose.

INTERVIEWEE: Exactly. So he wined and dined and had on his mind him becoming a citizen, which he did. And so that is how I got an Italian surname.

INTERVIEWER: Did they stay married?

INTERVIEWEE: Of course they did, for the first four years. She had three children and he had his papers, and children back in Italy to support. So the story goes. The lesson has been around for decades. The scenario is present history.

INTERVIEWER: Well, let it be known you are an important part of the history. Thank you, um, how do you pronounce your name again?

INTERVIEWEE: That's Margarita Balsecas Pignataro. But you can call me Maggie.

INTERVIEWER: Grassy ass Maggie.

INTERVIEWEE: Grassy ass? Yo, what you talking? Who has a grassy ass?

INTERVIEWER: (Smiles.) Don't worry, I'll tell them you are okay and they don't have to place you into that special white pajamas. I think you run around the room talking five accents a minute with spread arms as your wings because you are ready to fly south. I'll get you a separate room for creativity so you won't bother the others.

INTERVIEWEE: Gracias. ¿Sái qué? Even if you don't 100 percent understand me, you listen to me. But... don't you get tired of listening to the same thing, I mean, this is our fifth reunion together. How many more times you going to ask me the same questions? I mean, tomorrow I'll come back and this oral history lesson will be repeated.

INTERVIEWEE exits stage right.

Vida Mia García

THIS WILD TONGUE TAMED:
A MEMOIR, A EULOGY, A DIATRIBE, A PRAYER

> *"I overheard a Mexican American woman cashier in a busy cafeteria in El Paso tell her coworker to answer the phone by the cash register because she was too busy waiting on customers and the lights on the receiver 'estan blinkiando.' It was an old telephone with blinking lights for the different phone lines. I was paying for my food and saw the lights, then heard her say 'estan blinkiando,' so I knew I was home again."*
> - Ray Gonzalez, *The Underground Heart*

> *"In returning to the love of my race, I must return to the fact that not only has the mother been taken from me, but her tongue, her mothertongue. I want the language, feel my tongue rise to the occasion of feeling at home, in common. I know this language in my bones... and then it escapes me... 'You don't belong. ¡Quítate!'"*
> - Cherríe Moraga, *Loving in the War Years*

Like all good young urban hipsters, I have a profile on Friendster. I have set the access level at "unrestricted," so that anyone can view it and send me a message.

And one day, someone does.

It is brief, an introductory salutation and complimentary acknowledgement of my musical tastes. It contains a query about what other musical interests I might have.

And it is in Spanish.

Now, there is no reason why anyone shouldn't write to me in Spanish. My name screams—or perhaps coos—latinidad, my profile lists "rock en español" as my favorite musical interest, and my india-mestiza phenotype—for those inclined to read phenotypes as an index of... anything—is on full display in the accompanying photos. It is no great leap in logic for viewers/readers to assume that, yes indeed, I am Latina.

And Latina, apparently, means being able to speak Spanish.

Pos sí, claro, you might be saying. Or, perhaps equally likely: *well, duh. Being Latina means being able to speak Spanish*—and though many may never admit to it outright, the contrapositive is inevitably there as well, weighted, waiting: *not being able to speak Spanish means not being Latina.*

I would like that to be an unfair, or at least a hasty, assessment, but things like this happen so often and so unremittingly that it is instead simply an accurate one. Why else the monolingual missive? (*Being Latina means being able to speak Spanish.*) If my profile had been devoid of racial or ethnic markers, would I have received the same message, but in English? And are these my only options? Why not a message in Tex-Mex or Spanglish or Caló—or, cripes, even Nahuatl? What assumptions are operating here? (*Not being able to speak Spanish means not being Latina.*) What (specious) cultural logic is at work that equates ethnicity with language fluency—or, to put a finer point on it, uses fluency as a litmus of ethnic identification and solidarity?

I understand and empathize with the jump to Spanish as a means of building community, to huddle around a shared and sacred insider's knowledge that is continually denigrated from without. I feel this move in my heart. I spend most of my time lately wandering the campus of an elite, moneyed, overwhelmingly white institution. In this environment, how many times have my own ears pricked up at the sound of Spanish? How many times have I used Spanglish in a mixed crowd and refused to translate? How many times have I struck up a conversation in Spanish with the only other brown face in a room as a way of drawing battle lines? Strategic essentialism? You bet your culo; that Spivak was on to something. It is more than some effervescent sense of cultural camaraderie that compels us to establish these alliances (though, as a form of strategic essentialism it necessarily possesses a temporal aspect, and it remains significantly grounded in a sense of amity and kinship). Rather, this kind of Spanish is an invitation and an offering, its utterance a counterhegemonic gesture that jumps to conclusions in order to leap across lines of class, nationality, generation, gender, and sexuality.

And for you cynics out there (hey, I'd be one of them), this is also more than an attempt to breezily disavow relative privilege. I harbor no delusions about the vastly different social, economic, and political battles that grad students and janitors, faculty members and foodservice workers are each waging—as well as these battles' disparate material effects on our respective lives. There are limits to everything, including language. And so would you feel differently about my argument, about me, if I told you that the writer of that genial Friendster note was white? I bet for a lot of you, that changes things. I'll be honest: it did for me. I mean, the accompanying photo wasn't very clear, and far be it from me to make one of those phenotypic deductions, but I must confess to trying to piece together my Friendster's ethnicity from those pedacitos of personality.

Hometown: Lexington, Kentucky. *Hmm.* But I don't want to be geographically essentialist, so I go for something else.

Occupation: union organizer. *Well, geez—UFW or AFL-CIO?* Another maybe.

Of course, the only way to find out for sure is to respond, to begin a conversation that is sensitive to this individual's personal historical particulars. And so I respond. In Spanglish. I want to know which tongue this person will take. Which feels like home, English or Spanish? Or—¡eso!—would I get some Spanglish in return?

The response is again in monolingual Spanish—including the

information that "mis padres no me enseñaron español tampoco, porque eran gabachos."

Ah. White. "Gabacho," in his words, and I wonder if that's a pointed commentary on his parents' sociopolitical orientation, or if it's merely a convenient and funny descriptor. I am hesitant but curious—or, better, something in me wants to push the issue. So I continue to write back using a mix of Tex-Mex Spanish and English. He continues writing me in monolingual Spanish. Curiosity turns into wariness. What does he want? *Who* does he want? What does he expect of me? Why? I wonder if I am overreacting. I wonder if I should call him out. After all, this has happened before: how many times have I met white folks who, very shortly after our first acquaintance, express their excitement at *finally getting to practice my Spanish with someone!* And I am continually amazed at this presumption, at the sheer amnesia. How many ways do we already have of remembering it? Columbus, Cortes, the Middle Passage, Manifest Destiny, Guadalupe-Hidalgo, Plessy v. Ferguson, the Alamo, Wounded Knee, Tule Lake, Brown v. Board of Ed, Jim Crow, lynching, Prop 187, Prop 209, Gwen Araujo— how many more names do you need before you remember why I am what I am?

So I am willful. Spiteful. I want to burst that bubble. I want all their patronizing assumptions and imperialist nostalgia to spill forth so that they have to reckon with the (historically contingent) oddity in front of them: a Chicana who can't speak Spanish, a Mexican-American whose first and most fluent language is English.

So you want to practice your Spanish, ese? With who? Ain't nobody here but us pochas.

A brief (personal) history of global colonialism

As best as I can put it together, this is how it started:

Or no, not started. Too much credit.

Let me begin *in medias res*, turn origin into plot twist: half a million ago, some guys set out in a boat. They weren't the first to do it, and they wouldn't be the last, but they're the ones I'll concern myself with. Anyway, these men, these explorers or conquerors or mercenaries or imperial emissaries or Church missionaries—whatever we choose to term them—these men were looking for one place and stumbled upon another. And while this didn't exactly mesh with their original plans, these señores were nothing if not adaptable: some native know-how, coaxed out of the local populace by means various and nefarious; some weaponry; some vigorous displays of might makes right; some shrewd alliances; some promises of hellfire, some threats of eternal damnation; and some generous microbial assistance combined to effect (after a few centuries)... me. Us. La raza cósmica. Los hyphenateds. Mestizos, mulattos, half-breeds, hybrids, and border dwellers.

Oh stop now, you must be thinking. I know. Who am I, a brown girl, to make myself the telos of history? A brown queer girl, an epistemic center?

Fine. We'll start with my mother.

That's where it should have begun anyway, right? At home? I remember reading Cherríe Moraga's *Loving in the War Years* for the first time, her serrated prose pitching hard into my chest. Here was something that finally made sense, that spoke to and about facets of experience that had only been understood as fragments. Cherríe—and Gloria, and Barbara, and Suzanne, and all the others I would read in years to come—refused that fracture, insisting upon representing these pieces as interlocking, interdependent...

inextricable. What's more, Cherríe, this icon of Chicana feminism, was a self-professed half-breed who thought and wrote and loved in Spanish but was still anxious about speaking in Spanish. (Indeed, if there is any rueful acknowledgement of fracture in her work, it is here, in the aching disjuncture between mind and mouth, heart and tongue.) Her landmark essay "A Long Line of Vendidas" is a hybrid half-breed thing itself: part testimonio, part invective, part history lesson, part battle cry, puro corazón, pura mujer. It was a lifeline for me, to find my loss of language narrated, to find tangible proof that my existence wasn't anomalous or aberrant—that it wasn't, in some fundamental way, my own fault. I realized this reading the journal entry Moraga shares, recounting the frustrating experience of calling Berlitz to inquire about Spanish lessons. Angry and exasperated at both the agent on the phone and at the seeming absurdity of the situation, she ends her entry on a note of disgust: "Paying for culture. When I was born between the legs of the best teacher I could have had."

Eso.

For years I remained stuck on that sentence, unable to move past the bitterness it evoked in order to see the larger critique the author was making. Her resentment and ire are tied to notions of women's (cultural and physical) labor, labor that is materialized in a graphic image of blood, pain, and birth: the legacies of conquest playing out on the bodies of mothers and daughters. But what was for Cherríe a scathing critique of patriarchy and white supremacy, I could only understand as an indictment of my mother (and father) for failing to transmit that most basic and fundamental of cultural values. It was a reactionary response, yes, the defensive maneuvering of one who has finally found a measure of relief; now I could stop blaming myself... and start blaming them. (*My parents let me down! I never had a chance!*)

It wasn't until later that I began to ask them about their own experiences and motivations. And when I did, I realized that a process of partition had begun long before that of parturition.

Maybe it started in 1848. Maybe in 1836. Maybe in 1519. Ni modo. You see, Cherríe, in that space between your mother's legs you got closer to a mothertongue than I ever could have. In my case, I cannot claim even that most fundamental proximity.

Because did I mention that my family is from San Antonio, Texas (née San Antonio de Béxar, Tejas y Coahuila)? I mean, we're *from* San Antonio: our bloodroots extend deep there, three generations deep on each side. I have to reach back to my bisabuelos to be able to talk of border crossings of any sort—and even then, one branch of my family has "always" been in that area (the border crossed them, and all that). And so what I mean to say with all this is, we are three generations in the United States. In gringolandia. In Amerikkka. Three generations to acculturate—or be acculturated.

There are processes you are conscious of, and these you can fight.

There are processes you are conscious of, and don't want to fight.

I don't know when or where my antepasados began to draw the line, but they were surely spurred along by the sneers their Spanish elicited, the corporal punishment their children received, the countless psychic assaults that mark the daily lives of the Othered and the outside. And so I ask you: under these circumstances, what is giving up, or giving in? What is self-defense? And could you ever be presumptuous enough to render judgment on these (*not choices but*) decisions?

So my mother, it turns out, was not the best Spanish teacher I could have had. Not this Mexicana who never spoke Spanish growing up, who in fact didn't begin to learn the language in earnest until she was 20 years old. Too many precedents already set in place, their logic evident and inexorable. Cherríe's lament might have been my mother's, then, but it could never have been my own.

Perhaps if I had sailed out of my mother's body and into my grandmother's arms… oh, but not my mother's mother, who is fair-skinned and dyes her hair blond and calls herself Spanish and other Mexicans wetbacks.

Did my mother ever have a chance?

Three generations.

Despite all this, I know exactly what Ray Gonzalez is talking about. I know the sound of home. I know how home sounds different, how home sounds speak in a language unlike any other. Here are vocabularies of love, anger, power, prejudice—family grammars that for me have no English translation, even though I am well aware of their English counterparts. Because there is no homology, no commensurability between *mija* and "my daughter," between my mother's appraising *a ver* and the phrase "let's see." I know the lasting comfort and deep contentment found in a rasquache Tex-Mex tongue that continually shape-shifts and reinvents itself, that resists the dominant language surrounding it by appropriating and reforming it, then claiming it as its own. Yes. This is cultura, processual and dynamic. Contradictory and recursive. We do not have the luxury of seamless bilingualism; in its place, we forge new sounds and sites of home. *Parque el troque. Están blinkiando. Oye, y'all.* These are survival strategies. This is *ours.*

But then, I know exactly what Moraga is talking about as well. Too well.

La maestra está sobre el escritorio

It has not been for lack of trying. Understand that. I have wanted this tongue my entire life, have struggled since childhood to replace the clumsy dead weight in my mouth with a muscle lithe and lucid, as fluent in my mothertongue as it is in my mother's tongue. First and second grade at one of San Antonio's more progressive Episcopalian schools found me learning Spanish from a gringa teacher—only the first of many times I'd bear this indignity—her illustrated flashcards depicting scenes more utilitarian than realistic: short of unforeseen natural disaster, when would I ever have to declare that my teacher could be found on top of, or underneath, her desk? But we were game, all of us, and recited our prepositions in enthusiastic secondgrade singsong: *La maestra está sobre el escritorio. La maestra está abajo del escritorio.*

I'd come home wracked with near-paroxysms of pleasure, dying to show off what I'd learned. My tongue thrilled to feel the new familiar words, my tongue finally making concrete and tangible the sounds I'd grown up with in my (other) grandmother's kitchen. How could I know this language so deeply within, and still not know it at all? How could my tongue stumble even as it wrapped around those words in total recognition, the syntax and constructions falling neatly into place in my head? Still, I felt on the brink of mastery; gaining this knowledge made Spanish real, and speaking this knowledge made Spanish mine. Every day I learned something I already knew, and at seven years old I experienced this as utter affirmation.

Which makes what followed all the more awful. And effective.

I do not remember the first time it happened, only that it happened again and again in a slow but steady process of stigmatization (or what I know now to call "negative socialization"). I'd come home desperate to practice my Spanish, but instead of finding a proud and encouraging audience, I found only my father's derision. My Mexican father's derision. *Lah my-ess-trah estah sobray el ess-cree-torio. Lah my-ess-trah estah sobray el ess-cree-torio. Like that, mija?* All flat nasal whine and bolillo accent. As if to show me how ridiculous I sounded.

For a while my response was unfailing anger and righteous pique: *how am I supposed to learn if you don't take this seriously?!?* And I kept waiting for him to tire of the joke, for the day he would say, *Ya. Okay, mija—what do you want to know?* But that never happened. Not even with all the seven-year-old foot stomping and pouting, the only rhetorical devices I had to insist that, indeed, I was serious about this endeavor. And slowly, almost (but not quite) imperceptibly, my irritation turned inside out. Or, no—it turned outside in, the anger transforming into reticence and self-doubt: *maybe he's* not *joking. Maybe I* do *sound ridiculous.*

Lah my-ess-trah estah sobray el ess-cree-torio. Me, punctured, deflating. Collapsing into myself. *Lah my-ess-trah estah sobray el ess-cree-torio.* Him, mimicking, pitying. Smirking all the while.

Or wait, shit, I don't know. Maybe he wasn't smirking—maybe he was just smiling. Or maybe he was just being silly, my father with his affinity for nonsense and playful absurdity that marked the best parts of him. How do we know what we remember? How do we remember what we know? How is any interpretation I cast onto my recollections *not* tinged by retrospect; how is anything I write now, how is any sense I try to make now *not* colored by the person I am at the present moment: the things that I've learned, the commitments I claim, the precarious peace I have made with this man's death and absence?

I have been stitching together these memories, trying to create some sort of coherent tableau out of fragments with ragged ends and worn patches. An attempt to reconstruct dissolution. But what do I do when you are no longer here to ask? To indict? How do I wrestle with what you've created and the legacies you left behind? Because I will never know for certain what your reasons were. For a long time, I was too young to know to ask, and then for a longer time we did not speak in anything but hurled insults and objects. And when we finally began to fashion some alternative language, to communicate unarmed, he went and died on me. Sans deathbed epiphany and existential closure. So the best I can do now is piece together moments and plait them into context. Acknowledge all the things I do not want to remember, but will not let myself forget. This is my own recovery project.

And what I have come up with is this: my father did what he did out of fear. He was afraid—afraid that I would become *too* masterful, that I would take up Spanish effortlessly and become fluent, indistinguishable from native speakers. Not just indistinguishable; I would *be* a native speaker. I believe this prospect terrified my father.

It wasn't just the mimicking, you see. It was his continual anxiety around particular cultural markers. I see this now, as I excavate and (re)arrange. I read disparate incidents against each other:

I remember how, each time I transferred to a new school, my father would accompany me to registration to make sure I wasn't placed into any ESL, bilingual education, or even simply "Regular" classes. He would thunder at whichever hapless guidance counselor sat before us that I *must* be placed in an Honors or G/T class. Thunder. And I would sit silent, mortified not only at the scene he inevitably spawned, but by what I understood as the disdain and condescension implicit in his demand. I imagined the other mexicano parents and children around us hearing this discourse about placement and tracking as mere rhetoric masking his real declaration: *my daughter is better than that. Than them*.

But this I know in retrospect to be incorrect. Because these moments are always interwoven with the recollection of his embarrassed apologies: *I'm sorry, mijita, but I have to make sure. These Anglos see a Hispanic last name and they don't care who you are—they throw you into the remedial classes and forget about you.* And while some of that bore faint traces of elitism, a great deal more of it must be understood as yet another (self-)defensive response to a history of material and cultural dispossession. My father was not putting other mexicanos down; his defiant ethnic pride was evident in almost everything he did personally, professionally, and politically. Nor was he mindlessly parroting arguments that naturalize and legitimate educational stratification (a la, "some" people "deserved" to be in those classes, but not others). No. He was disparaging the ongoing, if not inevitable, ghettoization of ESL and Bilingual Education courses in a nation otherwise ideologically committed to monolingualism.

He knew. He had seen too much.

You see my father spent his entire career devoted to Bilingual Ed—to the idea, essentially, that full U.S. citizenship (in both the legal and discursive sense) is linked in significant ways to English (proficiency if not mastery). Therefore, ever the pragmatist, he acknowledged the necessity of English instruction for non-English speakers. But he also understood that being a U.S. citizen is not the same thing as being an American subject. It was not enough (it would never be enough) for us mexicanos to have access to education; we had to succeed in that arena, and not just succeed but excel. Surpass. As Hispanics, my sister and I had to be ten times better than Anglos—and as women, we had to be ten times better than men—in order to be seen as equals; these were the brute facts as my father figured them. And so we were raised to beat them at their own game.

For my dad, the master's tools may not have been the best implements for dismantling the master's house, but they made the destruction that much sweeter.

I understand if you are confused. I am too. It is a perplexing thing, the vexed and contradictory consequences of my father's life project: in defending against racist Anglo culture, my father inadvertently fended off vital aspects of Mexicano culture—even as he ceaselessly inculcated in his daughters a defiant pride in and sense of duty towards that culture. On the one hand, we were to be leaders, and were to take our privilege and return to the "Hispanic" community. It was our mandate as Hispanas, a responsibility that was ethnic and gendered and, as I see now, classed. But on the other, it seemed the only way to accomplish this goal was to alienate us from our community in profound and irrevocable ways.

I want you to appreciate the depth of irony here—as well as the depth of psychic violence involved. A violence Gloria Anzaldúa calls "linguistic terrorism" and links, significantly, not just to racism but to internalized racism: "because we internalize how our language has been used against us by the dominant culture, we use our language differences against each other." Could my father, true native speaker that he was, have foreseen this? Or did he comprehend the consequences, and deem them an acceptable cost?

I piece and plait and try to understand.

I still wonder if he meant to humiliate me with his mimicking. I wonder how much of the anxiety my burgeoning bilingualism elicited was conscious and nameable, and how much of it was inchoate and affective. Did it make him squirm, to hear me sound more and more like the students he was trying to teach English? Did he labor every day in the belief that English would open up doors of opportunity in the U.S., only to come home and find his work for naught, his progress in the classroom a stark counterpoint to his daughter's regression at home? Maybe he was trying to put me in my place before anyone else could; something along the lines of, *this is for your own good; better you suffer this at my hand, someone who loves you, than at the hand of...* The logic is twisted, yes, but somehow impeccable: it simply mirrors that of the racist crucible in which it was forged.

So that is how it happened in my family. The legacies of conquest played out in the psyches of fathers and daughters.

Enough is enough (it will never be enough)

> "So, if you want to really hurt me, talk badly about my language."
> - Gloria Anzaldúa, *Borderlands/La frontera*

In case you were thinking that I was constructing some facile binary in the beginning of my essay—when Latinos assume I speak Spanish, it's happy solidarity; when Anglos assume, it's racist amnesia—well, I've got another story for you. It concerns a phone call I fielded while staffing the office of a small nonprofit. A small, grassroots, radical leftist, feminist, queer, avowedly latinoamericana/o and particularly Xicana/o cultural arts organization.

Not that it mattered.

The woman on the other line began to speak in Spanish, then stopped and asked me if I spoke Spanish. I replied with the usual disclaimer: *Bueno, sí... lo puedo hablar, pero lo hablo todo mocho.* [Here I likely made some sort of self-effacing sound, part sheepish giggle, part wistful sigh. The usual self-deprecation sets in before anyone can beat me to it.] *Pero lo entiendo muy bien; si prefiere hablar en español, le puedo ayudar.*

Oh, no, that's fine, she replies. *We can speak in English.*

I cannot for the life of me remember what we discussed, only that our exchange was brief, and genial in a professional sort of way. Nothing seemed amiss; my defenses were down. Near the end of the conversation, she thanked me for my help and asked for my name.

Vida Mia, I offer chirpily.

There is silence on the other line. Then, *your name is Vida Mia? Are you Mexican?*

Uh-huh, I say cheerily—but already I can sense where this is going, the sharp turn we have taken, and the old familiar dread opens up in my stomach. This will not turn out well.

You're Mexican and you don't know how to speak Spanish?

I didn't say I didn't know. I said I wasn't great. And what kind of question is that? Does she really expect me to answer? Or does she expect me to justify myself? Do I even have a choice? Is there any response that wouldn't condemn me, confirm what is in her eyes my reprobate ethnicity? I am momentarily stunned, not by the indictment (which is so typical, and illogical, as to be laughable) but rather by the sudden viciousness, the disdain that borders on hostility; it is as if I have deliberately deceived her. But I have no idea who this woman is. She has no idea who I am.

What? Look, see, I—

She cuts me off. Midsentence she cuts me off and my tongue my tongue is left hanging, a bloody stump.

How can you not know Spanish? How can you call yourself a Mexican? What, don't you have any pride in your background? I would be ashamed if I were you. You should have more respect for your culture than that.

And with that helpful advice, she hangs up.

The drone of the dial tone snaps me out of my disbelief, and I am suddenly, wildly enraged. *How can I call myself a Mexican? What kind of question is that?* Who the fuck are *you*? Am I seriously being lectured by a stranger—blindsided in the middle of my workday, a workday spent advocating on behalf of out of love for Mexicanas/os—on suitable and proper cultural identity?

The only person I hate more than that woman is myself.

And so all my inclinations towards linguistic solidarity come crashing down, and I am forcefully reminded that language has its barbed limits. Just as it has the potential to cut across lines of class, nationality, generation, gender, and sexuality, language also has the ability to divide—to delineate and classify (who is "properly" Latina/o), to judge, and to rend.

Language lacerates. The oppressive regulatory functions that it performs operate within as well as on Latino communities, and both Latinos and whitefolk make all kinds of similar, and similarly ridiculous, assumptions about language ability. (*Not being able to speak Spanish means not being Latina.*) Of course, I understand why and how the roots of those assumptions may be different; I am sensitive to that. But seldom have I found similar consideration from native Spanish speakers. (Except for Cubanos, I must note; while taking Spanish classes in Havana, I was amazed at how many Cubanos apprehended the entirety of the statement, "Soy Chicana. De los Estados Unidos." Their understanding was immediate and sympathetic; "Ah sí, los chicanos. Ustedes entienden colonialismo también como nosotros. Les han robado su tierra y no les permitían hablar su lenguaje. Pero que bueno que estas aprendíendolo.") Instead, as that fateful phone call demonstrates, I often meet with native Spanish speakers' pity, hostility, disdain, and/or disgust.

Please tell me, those of you who have ever mocked or scorned another Latinos' tongue-tied Spanish: what exactly does this accomplish? You do understand this puts us in a bit of a double bind; you want us to learn the language, but ridicule and disparage our tentative or inelegant efforts. I can assure you that this response inspires neither confidence nor assiduous conversational practice. Yet perhaps there is an echo here of my father's curious logic: if Anglo cruelty was disastrously effective in shaming the Spanish out of us, mightn't Latino cruelty be equally effective in shaming it back in?

It was in her essay "How to Tame a Wild Tongue" where Anzaldúa wrote about language difference and internalized racism. *Deslenguadas*, she called us. "*Somos los del español deficiente. We are your linguistic nightmare, your linguistic aberration, you linguistic mestisaje, the subject of your burla.*" But why? Is it that we embody the fear of acculturation, our clumsy tongues making a painful colonial history corporeal? This formulation understands language and culture as continually in peril, not as dynamic and developing, and certainly not as something that can be recovered and strengthened—indeed, it precludes the possibility that a linguistic recovery project might be the very source of the cultural strength and pride so often ascribed to fluency.

Which is simply another way of saying, some of the most fist-in-the-air Chicanas and Chicanos I know are the deslenguadas. Are they just overcompensating? Or must we admit the possibility that their positive self-conceptions are in part the product of this struggle for a mothertongue? "Ethnic identity is twin skin to linguistic identity—I am my language," Anzaldúa writes. "Until I can take pride in my language, I cannot take pride in myself." For my part, I know I became Chicana at the same moment I accepted my faulty Spanish. I know my ethnic politicization happened at the same moment I asserted my right to claim Chicana not in spite of my stuttering pocha bilingualism, but through it. This faltering tongue is tangible evidence of our historical presence and continual struggle in this country.

And this is why it is so hard to let it go.

Months now, I have been working on this essay. Tentative and fearful. Afraid of the anger and sorrow that must inevitably be dredged up, faced, reckoned with. But somewhere inside me, I must admit, I'm even more afraid of letting that anger, sorrow, and resentment go. Who am I without it? What of me remains? For so long I have at once willfully resisted and desperately sought Spanish, have defined my relationship to this language via the twin poles of defiance and love. When I become fluent—and I am now more than proficient in Spanish, and have long been if you count all those moments when I successfully pushed the insecurity out of my head and off of my tongue—does the complexity of my linguistic history disappear? Or will it be borne in my americana accent, for those who hear it (and care to listen)?

This wild tongue is not tame. Ni tiene pelos. It slips and stumbles, pero también grita y canta. And for all those other aberrant appendages, it prays.

On May 15, 2004, as I was in the middle of writing this essay, La Gloria se falleció. I was shocked and deeply saddened when I heard the news, as I had been feeling her presence so powerfully beside me during the preceding weeks and months that I composed these thoughts. She is everywhere in this work, and her imprints are everywhere in me. *Que en paz descanse, maestra, luchadora, poeta, mujerona.*

Cecilia Isabel Mendez

EL TEATRO DE LA COCINA / DRAMA OF THE KITCHEN

I grew up in a bilingual home hearing, speaking, and responding to English, Spanish, and, inevitably as was my case, Spanglish. I am first generation Latina born in the United States, the daughter of Panamanian parents who are now permanently transplanted. To be bilingual is a heritage I am proud of and one of the greatest gifts I have ever known. Life, as a result, can be one of experiences of extremes on a daily basis. On the one hand, the perceived dissolution of identity, confusing for the varying codes of conduct, culture, and language required between worlds, perhaps most evidenced in those moments when I feel neither fluent nor articulate enough to express anything in English nor in Spanish. On the other (heavily weighted) hand, there are those times and spaces when I feel richly laden with vocabulary, sense of place, understanding, sentiment, and belonging. Navigation between comfortability and confusion always calls for adaptation, flexibility, and faith that these challenges equip me only in the most positive of ways.

I am deeply invested in exploring on literal and metaphoric levels the reality of language as a tool of power. I am especially invested in this as a bilingual person working, living, teaching, and creating within both English and Spanish speaking communities. My ongoing investigation of language in my art practice inspires many questions, among them: How does language allow us access into physical and psychological spaces? What are ways in which language is informative and transforming? How do the meanings of words change between contexts? How are words played with, manipulated, and combined to form new words and meanings? The constant inventiveness of Spanglish, for example, embodies these possibilities: words split and are reconstructed, verbs recreated, constructions reorganized, double meanings abound. I have begun to explore some of the intricacies of Spanglish and the attributes of English and Spanish in a series of drawings entitled *El Teatro de la Cocina / Drama of the Kitchen.*

My drawings of kitchen tools are metaphors for the ways in which English and Spanish are mixed to create new words, rhythms, and forms of speech. Ingredients are processed through kitchen utensils to create food in ways symbolic to how words are constructed and de/reconstructed between two languages to produce new words and meanings. Words, like foods, are spliced and diced, mixed, blended, weighed, recombined, and ultimately transformed. In language, as with image, there is much invention. I use appliances- like languages and words- to create sustenance for body and spirit on multiple planes at once physical, emotional, psychological.

For example, *al comprimir / upon pressing* and *exprimirdora / squeezer* refer to the challenging act of translating: a material enters a receptacle and emerges changed by virtue of its having passed through hundreds of holes, or filters. Likewise, exact translations between English and Spanish (or any two languages for that matter) are often lacking in sentiment, while translations that are true to the essence of a message are often not exactly literal. *midiendo la masa / weighing the maize* represents the weight words carry in different contexts, a skill useful in both multilingual and monolingual spheres. *amasando la masa / rolling the maize* speaks to the difference in general standards of beauty and effectiveness in two languages, with English often being praised when it is tight, edited, and concise while Spanish is stretched via its expansive vocabulary, known generally as a very 'flowery' language that inspires long and deliciously complex sentences. ***moledora moliendo / grinder grinding*** enacts through the body of a meat grinder the process of creating Spanglish verbs, formed by combining English infinitive verbs with the Spanish suffixes. *To park*, instead of being *estacionarse* becomes *parkear*. Seemingly infinite combinations of root words and verb endings create these hybrid action words. ***granulando / crushing*** refers to the power of the diminutive forms of speech so common in Spanish: the *–itos* and *–itas* attached to the endings of words. The pepper crusher takes a relatively large chunk of spice and pulverizes it, so as to imbue an entire dish with its flavor. Likewise, the *–ito* or *–ita* added to a word can imbue the sentiment in Spanish with much affection, or, depending on the delivery of the speech, a wide variety of emotions. ***batidora / beater*** and ***batiendo / whisking*** make jarring or swift back-and-forth actions, mixing materials that mimic the way phrases in Inglés y Español switch at times at a fast pace, cambiando one way y luego al otro to build full sentences, thoughts, phrases.

Finally, the corers in ***despepitándose por / yearning for...*** and ***despepitar / to core*** depict the digging for the seeds of a tomato—that is, it's essence, the source that affords the fruit its regenerative powers. This coring represents both the physical challenge and emotional yearning involved in wanting to understand content and context across languages and cultures: to grasp meanings and words, belong to a linguistic community, to be a part of. These themes have inspired the poem I have included in this portfolio of works, entitled ***despepitándose por (yearning for) el tomate: the word.***

despepitándose por (yearning for) el tomate: the word

birth of word / tomato / tomate:
fleshy, carnal, suave, aguado, claro, wet, lloroso, evaporado,
i'd like to nuzzle into your flesh, seeds and their aqueousness
surround your structure gelatinous
your core that a veces me falta
no me acuerdo the proper gramática
working back   and forth   across this gap
donde me pierdo...

Tomato: apple of gold- you can be so many things:
whole, wedges, pureé, chopped chunks, diced destined for as
many purposes:
un ajiaco, a stew, una salsa, un potaje, un guizado, a salad
all valid but so not the same thing...
your flavor explodes into endless codes
and so
we find ourselves
d / de / des / des-pe / des-pep
despep-i/ despepit / despepit-á
despepitán / despepitánd / despepitándos...
despepitándo-se...

despepitándose por,
yearning for,
     despepitándose por...
este baile, the dance between
two sides of a border ya brimming with both:
English   Spanish   and Spanglish is born

despepitándose por...
un fragmento, an utterance,
those bits of letters, spaces, on either side of a comma,
rush before an exclamation point, masses marching between
question marks.

despepitándose por...
tómate la palabra, the word, guiando por los guiones, steering
through hyphens, saltando, jumping over these fissures, gaps,
cracks, cradled spaces where i'm:

searing, buscando, investigando, struggling, luchando, héchan-
dole esfuerzo
and all i can come up with is:

'Cómo se dice / how do you say'
'Cómo se dice / how do you say'
'Cómo se say / how do you dice'
'Cómo se dice / how do you say…'

supercalifragilistic, expialadocious…

pues, no hay traducción mihija, there's no translation here…
so we mix it up, some say we end up hyphenized, traumatized,
ni-linguilized, bilingually exorcised,
language polluted,
this notion, sometimes refuted,
this question proposed:

to refuse- or ingest- the choking aromas
de tanto idioma,
tantas palabras machacadas, so many words masqueraded
terrón de dulce sweet y lumps of acid words paraded—
but how about…celebrated?

and so we return to the beautiful word:
Tomate, yes you, tomato
vasilando entre, wavering between
sy - lla - bles
tragando s's, rrr's, d's,
swallowing consonants, erupting vowels,
cantando alabanzas,
singing praises: your sweetness is bitter, your acidiy fresco fresh

so sink in sharp, or slow, let a short liquid flow,
y try, prueba, this bounce—es rico, rich
this trans-lation,
   -formation,
   -literation,
   -culturation,
   -exclamation:

   so ya, vente a comer; the sopa's ready, come and get it…

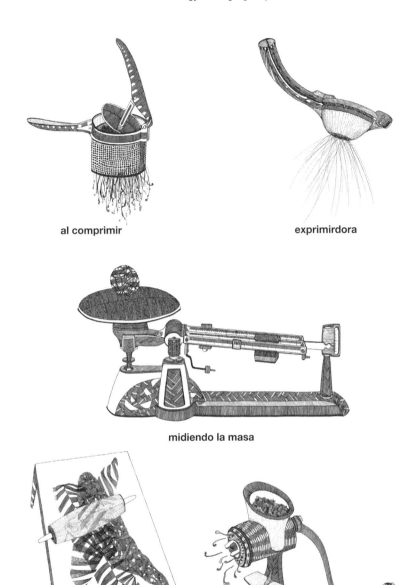

al comprimir

exprimirdora

midiendo la masa

amasando la masa

moledora moliendo

Illustrations © 2002 Cecilia Isabel Méndez.

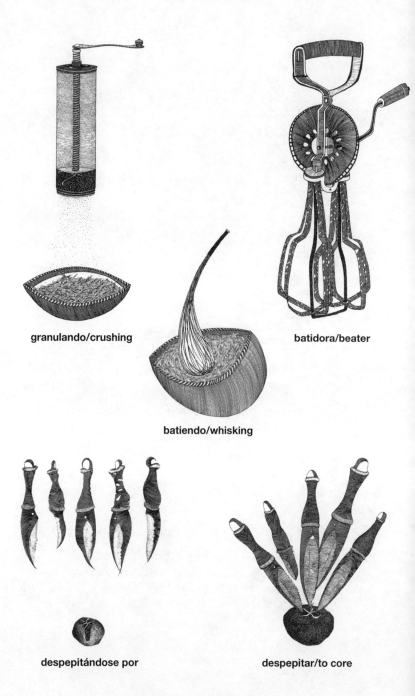

granulando/crushing

batidora/beater

batiendo/whisking

despepitándose por

despepitar/to core

Illustrations © 2002 Cecilia Isabel Méndez.

Cecilia Isabel Méndez

Melani Martinez

DUENDE PLAY

The rim of the wound

In the first several months of studying flamenco intensively, I started experiencing pain in my body. My ankles were sore, my hips were out of place, and my knees seemed to always feel like they could slip easily into hyperextension to the point of dislocation. Sometimes when I walked my knee would slip away from me for a split second. My joints and tendons inside would move away from the direction I had appointed them. They would move in their own way, and touch a place of near destruction. I was sometimes scared to move. I took joint complexes and found the money to afford a couple visits to an acupuncturist, but it relieved nothing. My knees continually went where they wanted without my permission. I was depressed, and decided to stop going to class. I considered quitting flamenco (after I had been studying and performing it progressively for nearly ten years) and making another life. After about a month, I returned to the studio, confused and depressed still, slipping on my flamenco shoes with pain and fear.

Federico Garcia Lorca wrote about duende—the hidden and telling part of us that we can awaken in art. In flamenco, duende should be released. It should be called upon by the performer whether dancer, singer, or musician, and in the mist of movement and poetry and music, it should speak. Lorca suggests that duende is our inner demon and causes us to suffer when played out. Duende plays the rim of our wounds, extracting our worst pang in little bites. It is, perhaps, some kind of pain ritual in order to bring about an understanding for the observer and the observed. You get up on stage in your best dress and lips painted and say, "This is what hurts me. Can you see it?"

I made an agreement with God once that if He would just relieve the pain in my legs and hips, that I would work as hard as I could on flamenco and that I would do my very best for Him. In the few years preceding, I had committed myself to flamenco, but had lapsed in my studies. I never practiced on my own. I didn't learn any songs. I simply did the least amount required—go to several classes a week, and occasional rehearsals. When I did start feeling a little better, I kept my promise for about two weeks. I fell back into my old routine of half-heartedness, and the pain continued on and off. A physical therapist told me that the injury would probably be something I had to live with for a long while, so I had to be adamant about icing and heating and stretching, and everything else. But the injury would move every few weeks— from my knees to my ankle, to one hip then the other, and then to lower back and back to knees. I just let it alone. When the pain would come, I would complain, but just let it alone. I came to the conclusion that maybe God wasn't going to take it away. Maybe it was a wound that was not ever going to heal.

Federico Garcia Lorca believed, as most flamenco aficiona- dos do, that flamenco is indeed an elite art form. In what other performance art do you incorporate poetry, music, and movement in a highly specified structure of improvisation, within complicat- ed rhythms stemming from a culture in oppression for the precise reason to express directly and fully the things inside of you? Well, maybe jazz. But Lorca suggests that only Spain is open to the power of duende. And without duende, art is suffocated. Flamen- co, for sure, is its own language—one that engages the energy of sung poetry and impressive percussion accompanying gesture and motion. Whether or not it belongs solely to the gypsies of Andalucia is debatable, and is in fact debated constantly. Lorca says that it is simply in the blood, and that people of Spain have the unique ability to be open to its facilitator — the duende.

Communion

I do not speak Spanish. My abuelitos claim that I spoke it when I was very young, but I don't remember any of that. I have made little effort to learn. While in Spain for a month, I listened to flamenco instructors give their very best advice, and I understood nearly none of it. I had nothing to say back. I cannot communicate in flamenco's inherent language. I attempt to dance without comprehending much of what is being said over me in song. I actually attempt to interpret it. I pick up all the pellizcos, and make stories out of it with my arms and legs and weight. But still, I can't speak. When my Tata asks me a question in Spanish, I answer in English, or ask him, "What does it mean?" "Say it again." I cannot speak. How can you say anything without speaking? Dios, porque Tu dames una voz? For what?

My husband and I were married on Dia de los Muertos, the day of the dead. Some of my relatives questioned why we would choose such a morbid Mexican holiday, the day after Halloween, no less. I figured that perhaps underneath their skin they didn't remember that they were descendants of Mexico - that they were the product of a culture who celebrated in great festivity a day to honor the people who went before us; people whose blood pumped through us. I knew my blood. I even romanticized its formation from the depths of an Aztec grave swept in sun burnt dust. Hadn't they ever imagined that?

Lorca said that only Mexico could hold his country's hand. "Everywhere else," Lorca explained, "death is an end." Then, the duende can easily visit us too. It can play out our little human aches, our minuscule cuts and bruises. It is in our blood to embrace death and celebrate the earthly life. We know the earthly life is so full of precious mistakes and exquisite flaws. We make such perfect humans. And it is in us, too, to reach death - life's ultimate defeat—just to touch the breath of God; to be out of the world, and closer to Him. Lorca says this openness to death is what makes the very attempt to communicate with God through duende possible. It is an unexplainable enigma of prayer. We can only talk to God if we know that we will fail trying.

I agree to perform a solo flamenco piece in a show, and then proceed to ignore all the practice and creation of choreography required for me to dance well and to my satisfaction. I find excuses to not rehearse. I refuse to walk into the studio on my own. Instead, I go home and worry about it. Others spend hours rehearsing the second they know they have the opportunity to perform. They file into the dance studio rooms and work together their steps and variations. I stare into the mirror for a few minutes. Then leave. I get frustrated. I misunderstand the words in the songs. I misinterpret the aire—the tone. I make claims and retire to the television set. Whatever I make, I won't like. Even if it feels good, I won't like it. I will fail. Always, I will fail. Miss the mark. Slip. Sin.

Duende, according to Lorca, produces a religious enthusiasm. A bug. A hook. You get it, then you can't stop thinking about flamenco for five minutes. You quit your job. You dye your hair sharp black. You reverse your lifestyle. You move away from your family and you pursue a career in the flamenco arts.

I did all of that. And somewhere in my change I realized what it costs. What it asks of you. Then I decided that I could keep it at bay. I could act as if it isn't that important to me. I could quit whenever I wanted. I would sip from it slowly, once or twice a day. No more. But duende asks for everything. It asks to be the first in line. It promises to caress you and help you talk to God. You get hit harder after. You remember all the things you hated about yourself. You remember your childhood. Then on stage, in full adornment, it subjects you to horrendous pain. You think you can just let it come, then manipulate it for the audience. You can't. You are not the craftsman. You are the tool. And I am a poor one at that. I have trouble conveying messages. My own voice fights for space on stage and any clarity is lost. I can't even speak the right language. And so, when I dance my poetry happens in my own head and I mesh it with the sounds of the words that I don't understand. Sometimes I think of nothing. Sometimes I think of my Nana dead in her grave. Sometimes I think of lonely people. Sometimes I think of the love I have that I can't explain. Sometimes I think of God and wonder if he can forgive me for loving myself more that I love others, and for wanting flamenco so much that I push it all away.

My Nana tried to teach me Spanish when I was young. Forty-five minutes a night of writing down words and their Spanish counterparts. I ended up with long lists of descriptions and objects and body parts. I never got to verbs. There was never any action on my loose-leaf paper. At the end of each lesson she'd send me off to bed. If I couldn't sleep, I was allowed to stay up with her and pray the rosary. We would sit together in the dim living room light with the television on but no sound; her fingers running over golden spheres, mine on glow in the dark plastic. It made me sleepy almost every time. When I turned twelve I decided that she was a pain and didn't talk to her much more. The lessons, of course, ended. I have read that second and third generation Latinos fail to retain Spanish as a spoken language. I am fourth generation. I am the depleted source. I was the one who decided I was too good to sit with the very woman who could have enabled me to speak. She died before I had any thoughts about needing what she could have passed to me. She left before I could realize that she might have been my only chance to learn Spanish the way my family speaks it. No one else tried to teach me, and she is never coming back.

In the End

I was fifteen years old when I first saw a dead person. My Nana was resting in her mechanical bed in her room full of scentless air. She was dead and I saw her body, but I could no longer see her. She hadn't spoken for about a month before she died. Perhaps there was nothing to say. My mother said that I could talk to her—that she might still be able to hear me. But I couldn't speak. I whimpered and that's all. Nothing was said. I knew then, for sure, that I would die someday, and that at some point I would end my trials here in this way.

Then duende was available to me.

It seems unlikely that one could explain the value of the art of flamenco by describing the physical details of its movement. The curve of the hands, the precise posture, or rapid twists and heels. The literal phrases will not illustrate the depths of what happens when good and honest artists take the stage and play out their insides. It is an abstraction. It is difficult to describe the essence of a painting by outlining the path of the brushstrokes.

I look and see the sweat in the air. We are working.

My friends feel nervous and sit firmly in their seats beside me. The bright material sticks to us.

In the light.

In the shadows are the men wearing black with their fingers curled and their dress shoes scraping the floor. They have sat with me in drunken squalor as I told my secrets by a fire or at the wheel of a car.

We laughed.

When the hollering and pounding breaks us from the normal day we were all having the audience is pleased. Many of them are my friends too. They stare and stare and sit high on their seats waiting for a piece of their own hearts to shed skin. In the middle is the one who will let us see it. Let us see it all.

He can tell us what to be and how to feel and on the sides, we can feel what it is for chests to collapse or necks to be thrown back.

One of us will be next. And then another.

We will mull over the floor and drop ourselves so that we can be lifted out. Everyone pushes us to be lifted out.

It gets silly, and then we remember our normal day. We put on our normal shoes and our normal face and go home.

I find that I cannot quit. Flamenco becomes family and freedom and reasons to have babies and tell stories. Ridiculous fears and back pain—my own psyche—they feed it. They make me remember that I can leave it in its place, but I can't just leave it. I have a tie to its blood, and a right to its expressive potential, and Lorca can know that in his grave. He can fit it into his poetry and then I will read it. In English.

Rosie Molinary

THE LATINA IN ME

The Latina in me is frustrated. She stays awake late and contemplates marriage and feminism while my gringa sleeps. I never fought this battle before, not until my friends started marrying and producing children, and my Latin mother started suggesting marriage to the man I consider her "Great White Hope."

Mamacita has been praying for a husband for me for far too long. She lights candles and recites rosaries for her hijita soltera.

"Don't ask for an esposo in my name," I implore.

"Y que?," she replies.

"Pray for starving children. That's the type of prayer for which you call upon God. Do that in my name."

"Oh si?," she challenges, and I see I have done nothing to alter her agenda except add a whispered postscript for good measure to make this hijita less spitfire y mas feminina.

I figure it goes like this: I, the multi-ethnic child of Latino parents and American upbringing, should be able to take from my culture what I need and then add anything else as I go. A little bit of MTV here, some pizza there, football on Thanksgiving, winter flurries, a lifetime without dresses or make-up, and dating early without the parental inquisition. Throw that all in with the Taina in me: the loud music, spicy foods, long embraces, energetic dancing, Spanish speaking, decibel shattering conversations, and extended family tree and there you find me, as Americanized as the Native Americans: colonized, yet fighting the conqueror.

But, then, that was me figuring it out nice and neat and convenient, and the one thing I've learned in this America (that a good ole boy will gladly remind me is not mine to claim) is that there isn't much here that is nice and neat and convenient. Not all at once, anyway, unless I am counting on billboards advertising truck stop restrooms on I-85 to give me truth. I am not, and my ethnicity has affected my self-concept too much for me to ignore it. The Latina in me finally has to make peace.

Mamacita wants me married. We ignore this truth as if it might somehow be less apparent the more that it's downplayed. I am wrecked not just by her idea that marriage will be my salvation, but by the hope that it will give her, an assurance that marriage and children will make me the Latina that I have never been. I have always been too certain for her, too independent. I try to ignore her disappointment in my casual appearance, my autonomy, my dismissal of the importance of men, marriage, and children. She will not accept that my desire to take care of myself is not in spite of my Latin culture; it is not an indication of my Americaness.

I feel this way, but then I consider the Americans I know, how most see me as just like them, and I am stuck, stranded, struggling to figure out how I became an Anglo without any birthright. Ultimately, with the dismissal of my otherness, I stifle my voice.

I have always faltered in conversation, struggled with what I wanted to say and what I could not say. My frame of reference, first generation Puerto Rican girl in the American South, never found company for reflection. It began at home where I did not have the words in Spanish to explain to my parents what it meant to be seen as un-American when my citizenship was just as valid as the blonde-headed boy sitting next to me in Social Studies. But he didn't agree, and he spat at me later, phlegm and hatred wrapped in one. I shook as I confronted him, terrified that I would not find the words to tell him that I had worth, that I did not belong working in his kitchen, that I could participate in his world, or any other that I chose. I told myself that I did the right thing, that my words had been right, that the world was indeed open. But I had no one to turn to who might understand. There was no one with whom to commiserate, and I battled to discover when and how to offer my voice.

Not until those pre-teen years did I begin to understand that because of my skin tone, I might be categorized without my consent. In the dark and musty hallway of my sixth grade building, I fumbled with my locker. I was tan from the summer. My black hair hung over my eyes as I wound the lock in each direction. A girl with a long and wild rat tail candidly asked as she walked by me, "Are you mixed?" I struggled to understand what she meant, how she might see me as "mixed." She re-worded her question several times and, finally, she settled on the blunt and blatant; "Is your daddy black and your momma white?" It was South Carolina in the mid-1980s and heritage mattered as much in friendship as kindness and decency.

I explained about Puerto Rico, our homeland in the Caribbean. She stared at me, vacant and dissatisfied, willing me to stop speaking so that she could offer what she thought.

"You gotta be one or the other, white or black. I'm just gonna call you white 'cause you're smart."

That was it. She closed her locker, walked off content, and later even asked me to spend the night. The exchange was complete for her and, yet, numbing to me. I had no desire to be white in her eyes or anyone else's. I wanted my own definition, wanted to be seen in the way that I saw myself: a first generation Puerto Rican trying to create her own way.

As I grew older, the severity of the things that I could not tell my parents intensified. Previously, others denied my heritage because they did not understand my ethnicity. Now, people denied me opportunity because they felt that they knew my ethnicity.

Immigrant families experience the parenting role awkwardly shift away from the parents, who struggle to simultaneously learn language and culture while providing for their family, to the children whose adaptability allows more rapid assimilation and language acquisition. I worked hard to protect my parents from this element of America. I wanted for them to feel satisfied with their decision to stay here. I wanted to keep the suitcases from coming off the shelves, the For Sale signs out of the yard. I wanted America, the only home that I could remember, despite the fact that not all of her people wanted me, so I learned to protect my parents from what no one wanted to believe could happen here.

I never told my parents that the Guidance Counselor, who reviewed my perfect report card, wished to remove me from Honors classes and enroll me in Work Readiness courses. My file differed in one way from my peers in the Talented and Gifted Program. It read Puerto Rican.

Shocked, I left his office, and stumbled down the hall to another counselor who saw that I had worth and added me to his own caseload. Years later, he encouraged me to apply to multiple colleges, waiving my application fee. "Let's see how we can do," he smiled as I nodded, and my Latina took on the challenge, tempering a stewing vindication she still needed from the first counselor as she completed the forms.

When I wasn't judged for my ethnicity, I was denied it. In English class, I was told that I was not Puerto Rican because I was not like the other Puerto Ricans, because I was neither pregnant nor strung out like the "Reekins" that this girl in my class knew.

In her world, if I didn't have track marks, I couldn't be from the Caribbean. My face grew hot as I argued, the same anxiety that visited me years earlier with the spitting boy, the rat tail girl, and the narrow-minded counselor haunting me again.

This denial rendered me silent, frozen on the borderlands between my Latina and my gringa, wondering which face to look to or turn from in order to find myself. In college, a friend omitted my ethnicity as we talked about my upbringing. We were talking about the rules in my family that were based on God, culture, and machismo.

"You are not a gringa," my mother would tell me after she forbade me from sleeping over with friends or cruising the mall. I would shuffle back to the phone, figuring out how to explain what I considered irrational reasoning to my friends who I did not want to dislike my parents. My friend eyed me as I retold this story.

"But you aren't really Puerto Rican," she insisted.

Why did she believe this so absolutely? Why could she say what made up my whole? How was I betraying my truth?

Those were the things that once forced me silent. I believed that no one wanted to hear what I had to say, and so I never said it. My parents couldn't understand what I had to say, so I never explained it. Ultimately, I learned that the issue was more often about vision than about words. It was about how people define what they see, and how I saw myself.

Later, the Latina mystique chilled me most. Some men find me sexy and beautiful, alluring and free game not because I am those things, but because I am ethnic, a girl from the Island, a Latina who must be able to make love in a whole new way.

In my twenties, as a teacher clothed in long skirts and baggy sweaters, I, inevitably, elicited a sexual reaction from students when I mentioned my ethnicity. At twenty-two, on my first day with a new class, the football players slapped high-fives and affectionately started calling me their "Puerto Rican Pecan."

I struggled to understand the nickname, why my male students loved to say it, why they snickered as they said it. Was it the alliteration that was so enticing? I convinced myself that it was the sound, that they were impressed with the music of the chant, until I overheard one whisper to another, "Man, our Puerto Rican Pecan makes me want to blow a nut." It stunned me, numbed my understanding of my ethnicity, made me wonder if I should go on embracing my roots or ignore the part of my identity that might make me seem sexy instead of intellectual.

As I became a more bold authority figure, I learned I had to sometimes shield the side of me that was hip, young, and vibrant. As the star basketball player walked into class one day, I congratulated him on his game the previous night.

"You worked hard. Congratulations."

He looked me over in a way that no man had ever looked at me.

"You can give me a massage if you want to congratulate me," he answered.

"Sit down," I retorted, trying to be harder than I was, "you and I both know that's not happening."

What was it about me that made him cross the line? Why did my students ask me to prom, look me up and down, inquire about my private life, wonder aloud if I was sleeping with the other soccer coach? What was it about me that was so sexual to them when my own life seemed so asexual?

As a teacher, I wanted to claim my ethnicity in order to empower my students to celebrate their own heritages. I could "pass" as white, but I had never wanted to, and, finally, I thought that I controled a forum where, with my lead, nobody would have to pass. We could all just be who we wanted.

Maybe my idealism fell short. While my students did not hold the stereotypes that my peers had when I was in school, they had different opinions of what being a Latina might mean. Within minutes of telling them my ethnicity on the first day of class that first year, a young man asked at what age I became sexually active. I squinted my eyes at him, tempering my words. Another young man stuttered towards a new question.

"I mean, we was just wondering if you is sexually active now."

"Is that anywhere close to appropriate?," I asked, defiant.

"Would you ever get with one of us?"

I looked at them, head-strong, staring away their hopes of sex with me.

In the teacher's lounge, I swapped stories with other young, single teachers. These women were attractive, intelligent, fun-loving. They never mentioned their students propositioning them. I came to interpret the line of delineation as based on race. My colleagues were white, my students African-American. In my students' eyes, I represented two things: the crossroads between the white and black worlds and a local version of the sexy women that they lusted for in hip hop videos filmed on location across the Caribbean.

It was as if my latinness insinuated sensuality and sexuality. I was a myth and not a woman, Wyclef Jean's Maria to all these wanna-be Don Juans. It seemed that my womanhood meant sex and sensuality more than any other woman's, as if I could simply exhibit my breasts and never my mind and no one would be the lesser for it, as if by my very ethnicity I was promiscuous and un-educated, as if I was created to procreate.

Years later, I do not know if they saw me as some fledgling Jennifer Lopez. I am not certain if they were enraptured by my ethnicity or by my candor. Did they feel free to say these things because I was open and honest, without crossing the lines of professionalism that I carefully drew? Did they do these things because I was Puerto Rican or because of who they perceived me to be, without regard to how my ethnicity shaped my world-view and their view of me? I cannot answer, but I know that my experience with these propositions and chants, with these questions and challenges, forced me to look at my Boricua in a way that I never had.

Now when I walk New York City streets, (the one place where a young man will scream out, "Hey, Boricua, over here," where my Latina has never failed to be recognized, where I am still not certain that I am Latin enough and the random greetings from my homeland leave me simultaneously thrilled and intimidated), I see women who bought into the myth about our sexuality. They are riveted by the fixed illusion of what being a Latina might mean.

"It means nothing," I want to shout.

But that's not true. There have been times when it meant too much to me, and I cannot escape those memories, so I swallow my words and keep company with my latinness.

I started college with a 34-23-34 figure—black hair, full lips, round breasts all packaged in a sun tan and lip gloss, distinctly different from most women on campus. I met Christopher within weeks of my arrival. He approached me one evening after a meeting, and we were both captivated. I learned later that he shared my Puerto Rican heritage and Southern upbringing. He was tough-er than most guys I knew, and the toughness intrigued me and brought out my own edge. Because I was petrified by what I felt and acutely aware that falling for him would mean I would have to make tough decisions about privacy, intimacy and sexuality, I pretended to care less for him than I really did.

I was in my dorm room on an unusually warm February night. My phone rang, and I considered not answering it, embarrassed that I was in on a Saturday.

"Hello," I semi-whispered, bored, and a little blue.

"It's Christopher. Can you help us with Andre? He's really drunk and keeps calling out your name. I think your being here is the only thing that will get him to pass out."

"I won't tell you how that sounded," I replied, a smile warming my face. "I'll be right over."

Andre was also Puerto Rican and had developed a crush on me that I attributed to the solidarity he felt with me. As I left my dorm, I thought about Christopher's request. Andre was militant about his ethnicity, and it crossed many lines when he drank. I could imagine Christopher, a loyal friend who was smaller than Andre, pushing him out of whatever fraternity house was about to see trouble so Andre could avoid the possible expulsion from school that always hovered over him.

In Andre's room, I found Christopher and Stan, Andre's roommate, holding Andre down on the couch.

"She's here," Christopher relayed when he saw me.

"Where is she?"

I walked over to the couch and sat beside Andre, gently bringing my hand to his head.

"What do you need, buddy?" I whispered.

"Play Mariah," Andre sighed, and Stan moved over to the stereo to accommodate him. Hearing Mariah's voice lilt over the speakers, Andrew closed his eyes.

"Play Fantasia." His fingers traced the notes of the music in the air. This was the vulnerable, gentle, romantic side of Andre that always surprised but moved me, too. This side danced salsa and merengue with me, made me homemade chicken noodle soup when I was sick, bought me expensive jewelry that he would not take back, sent me what I referred to as "Miss America" roses.

Christopher moved to the VCR and popped in the video. Andre settled into the couch, his hands crossed over his barrel-chest. His breathing steadied, a soft snore off-beat with Mariah's voice. Christopher, Stan, and I relaxed, the two of them exhausted from putting Andre to bed. I moved to the arm of the couch.

"Thank you," Stan offered.

"I didn't do much," I replied, and the couch shook as Andre jumped up, sickness bleaching his face.

"I'll take him," Stan said, grabbing Andre's arm and leading him out to the restroom.

Christopher and I starred at the door, listening to them stumble down the hall, acutely aware that we were alone.

"Hey girl," he moved to me, and I looked at him, shyly. My eyes tracked over his caramel-colored skin, chocolate brown eyes, ebony hair, and the mole on his face.

"You did great." He slipped his fingers under my chin and tilted it towards him. I closed my eyes for a moment and then reopened them to find him pressing towards me, surprising me with one of many kisses that I would replay for years. We would argue about this kiss for the rest of our friendship, the debate of who kissed whom never settled.

Stan and Andre stumbled back to the room just as we pulled away, embarrassed. We both wiped our mouths, erasing any complicity.

"I can take it from here," Stan reassured us as Andre collapsed back onto the couch.

"You sure?" I asked, looking for anything to keep me from confronting what had just happened.

"Yep."

Christopher held the door open for me. Outside, we stumbled over idle conversation on the path that led to my dorm and the fraternity houses.

"Come out with me," Christopher pleaded, and in that moment, our pattern would be born. I wanted nothing more than to be out with him. But it terrified me, too, the list of possibilities such a decision would create. I perceived Christopher and me as mismatched and so I didn't try to match him, despite our affection for each other.

I clung to the myth that I had of myself as a sweet, innocent, unpassionate girl, which was central to my self-understanding. It was who I allowed myself to embody. Calling on that girl became a habit of mine that emerged in multiple possible relationships after him.

"I can't." I whispered, placing my hand on his arm, and then slowly backing away. My fingers touched the inside of his forearm as long as I could before the distance became too much.

Over the years, I battled this intense attraction. I wanted him desperately, but I was terrified of that wanting, unsure of what it meant and how to control it if unleashed. The risks that I was willing to take with him were barely physical or emotional. We kissed in private places, and I'd casually walk away. He shared intimate details of his life that he had never told anyone. I could rarely match his candor. I was terrified of being direct, of telling him what I felt, of being vulnerable. He sensed my withholding, both physically and emotionally, and confronted me on a beach one summer in Puerto Rico, the irony of both of us in our homeland working with orphaned children and denying our own abandonment issues not hitting me until years later.

Our world operated in the shadows of night, and I saw the women he was with in the day time. I felt smaller, sweeter, too clean cut, too plain. I couldn't imagine him dating someone so inexperienced, and, yet, each time that I was with him in private, I defied my understanding of myself. As I aged, I became risky, unaffected, confident, upbeat, sexy. In some weird twist of fate, I replaced the toned down parts of me with more apparent traces of my Latin culture. We both grew to love this woman who was sassy, fun, and confident, and he wanted as much of her as he could get. I did, too.

We never dated, as much as we watched each other across rooms, took long drives and spilled secrets, called each other from foreign countries, visited across state lines; we never made our relationship official. But over time, he made me believe that there was something infinitely sexy in the way I worked ceaselessly for my passions, in my Puerto Rican heritage, in my pseudo-edge and confidence, in my self-sufficiency and independence.

He moved on through women I considered needy, and I wondered, afterwards, if I had gotten it right. Clearly the edge had not won him over, and, while he had found it attractive, he had not found it compelling. He asked once,

"What if we had ever dated? Could we have made it?"

I paused before I answered, knowing that no matter what I said, we could not get our history back. I would never feel his hand on the small of my back again, guiding me through a room and telling me how beautiful or intelligent I was. We wouldn't kiss in inappropriate places, at inappropriate times, anymore.

I stared at him, horrified that I might reveal the depth of my affection for him.

"We wouldn't have made it. You need someone who is higher maintenance than me."

I walked off before I could hear him say "You're right."

He had always fallen for women who needed him, who defined themselves through him. I did my own maintenance. I perceived that I had no needs to be met by someone outside of myself when really I was just beginning to understand boundaries and react to them. I was so sturdy, so rational, so stable. Romantic passion was not any of those things and that frightened me.

I coached myself to compete in his world, to go match for match with him. While I didn't need him to define me, I was no more self-sufficient than the woman he would end up loving, but I had strapped on such severe latinness with an American flair that he could not detect my faultlines. He forged the metal to my steel-wool edge, made me brave enough and strong enough to alter how I approached the world. But, in order for us to have made it, I needed to have learned bravery before him.

For years, I never accurately perceived myself because I was waiting for it to come from someone else. I was waiting to always be a Latina or always a gringa, to always be pretty or always be plain, to be exotic or ignored, to be exciting or unalluring. I wanted a constant but never found it. The reactions to my looks, my reality were always extreme. I was waiting for external consistency to garner my own confidence. Ultimately, I realized that the only consistent view that I would get would be my own. My glance in the mirror would have to be accurate. I would have to respect my own assessment. My self-confidence would teach others how to interpret me so I did not have to make a sacrifice. The most important issue was not how other people defined what they saw, but how I defined what I felt, the way I melded my parts, and, thus, how I let my Latina and gringa each have her own voice.

Maybe, here, I find the root of my fear of marrying: this idea that with marriage I might finally become something that fits into a box of understanding that I have never experienced. In the past, I could never be just Puerto Rican because it rivaled what others defined as Puerto Rican, but I could also never be just a white or black girl because I countered those definitions as well. I was a shape-shifter, transcendental, a mirage. And I fell in love with the not belonging, the mystery, the freedom from place. But what if marrying changes all of that, gives me a club, the way that my mother hopes that it might? What if marriage precludes place and leaves me stranded in a one dimensional world of wife, far less vast, rich, and decadent than the lives I have been able to try on until now?

There is my fear: I will sacrifice my identity in marriage. The price of the union will be me. I do not want to become a full-time cook, maid, chauffeur, and beauty queen. I hate that some Hispanic formula of femininity, coupled with the cult of domesticity, makes some women into pawns who have no idea what hit them, or that they've even been hit at all. I imagine that is why my Latina is awake way past midnight, and my gringa sleeps soundly through this inner turmoil. The Latina, a Latina cut from a different mold than the one my Mamacita would like me to try on and from a different mold than my teenage students think they know, is keeping vigil for the next life to come. What will this woman allow for me, she thinks? Will others keep missing me when they look in my face, or will I finally be recognizable?

It seems, lately, that la isla is barreling down on my American upbringing as if it might be the end. Get a diamond ring on her finger, my mother must be thinking, and she'll come back to our team. But I am not the standard gringa nor am I the traditional

Latina and, finally, I know how to unite my guise.

I am the union of my parts. The truth is that every woman can be saccharin and salt, beauty and brawn, gentle and razor sharp. The wedding ring, Mamacita, changes nothing that I don't want it to change. From the very beginning, I had it right. I, the multi-ethnic child of Latino parents and American upbringing, am able to take from my culture what I need.

Luis Larios Vendrell

MI PADRE

Acabo de dejar a mi amiga Charlotte en su casa. Mientras vuelvo a la mía, me he puesto a pensar en otras tardes, hace, ahora, muchísimo tiempo, en que mi padre nos llevaba a los dos a comer hamburguesas. Eramos, entonces, muy niños, pero recuerdo la felicidad que sentía en el coche cuando nos dirigíamos al pequeño restaurante cercano a nuestra casa. Mi padre nunca pedía nada para él; de vez en cuando comía algunas de mis patatas frítas. A veces yo le daba un sorbito de gaseosa; me decía que le recordaba la que bebía de chico en España.

Había nacido en tierras castellanas, en una familia con dos hermanos que fueron, posteriormente, muy diferentes a él. Aunque amaba mucho a su patria creo que nunca se sintió a gusto allí. Fue extranjero hasta en su propio país. La opresión política y religiosa que padecía España en su juventud le afectaron poderosamente. La repentina muerte de su madre desbarató el orden y la esencia de aquella familia. Durante varios años deambuló por Europa sin rumbo. A los pocos años de vivir aquí, conoció a mi madre y se casaron en unos meses.

Mi padre era alto, bastante grueso, calvo y con ojos azules como yo. Siempre me pareció muy fuerte y yo admiraba todo lo que podía o sabía hacer. Le gustaba pasar mucho tiempo conmigo y frecuentemente, íbamos con mi perra "Reina" a las montañas. Me incitaba constantemente a hablar en español, y pronto descubrí que, en realidad bajo las máscaras de los dos idiomas, se ocultaban dos personas completamente distintas. En aquella época vivíamos en una casa muy grande de ladrillo rojo. Mi padre construyó un taller en un rincón del gigantesco jardín y allí pasamos juntos muchas horas inolvidables. Una de mis primeras palabras, al empezar a hablar, según me contaron más tarde fue: "torno" pues papinico - como le llamaba yo entonces - había conseguido uno y en aquel taller, los dos juntos lo montamos y, posteriormente cuando ya era yo un poco mayor, reconstruimos el motor cuando se quemó.

Mi padre leía mucho. Si cierro los ojos le veo leyendo en algún sofá de la casa. En el coche siempre tenía un libro y en una ocasión me dijo que no le gustaba no tener nada que hacer mientras me esperaba al venir al colegio a recogerme. Yo era entonces muy descuidado y muchas veces, me olvidaba completamente que mi padre me estaría esperando a la salida de mis clases.

Frecuentemente él y yo íbamos a ver a sus amigos o a algún negocio. Él era muy estricto conmigo y cuando se enfadaba me daba miedo y me era imposible reaccionar lo que le enojaba más. Sin duda fue por su carácter que mis padres se separaron. Al principio apenas se notaron grandes diferencias en nuestras vidas. Mi hermana y mi madre parecían evidentemente muy contentas, pero yo sentía un gran vacio al ir al taller y ver que no estaba allí, y comprender que ya nunca más volvería a verle. Eventualmente nos mudamos a una casa mucho más pequeña en un barrio sin árboles donde no conocíamos a nadie. Mi hermana tuvo que dejar de tomar clases particulares de piano, pero no creo que eso la preocupara mucho. Durante meses no supe nada de mi padre; yo al jugar con un avioncito de madera que me había construido en el taller sentía identificarme con él y no me importaba la distancia que nos separaba.

Un buen día supe, accidentalmente, que se había marchado a Alaska. En la biblioteca del colegio busqué un atlas y así comprendí lo lejos que estaba de mi padre. Por aquel tiempo leimos en mi clase de literatura americana un cuento escrito por Jack London que se desarrollaba en Alaska y en el que el protagonista moría de frío en una espantosa y desoladora soledad. Sentí una tristeza enorme y me puse a llorar; la profesora, creo recordar que era la Sra. Ortiz, me dejó que saliera al patio, y allí al volver a sentir el calor otoñal, me pareció mucho más injusto que mi padre estuviera lejos de mi experimentando aquel frío glacial.

La profesora debió llamar a mi madre pues, cuando llegué a casa nos sentamos y tuvimos una larga charla. Me preguntó si estaba todo bien; casi estuve a punto de decirla lo que había pasado y lo que sentía, pero luego comprendí que no lo entendería y sería una perdida de tiempo. Mi madre y yo raramente hablabamos; teniamos, eso sí, una comunicación superficial. Hasta cierto punto, ahora lo comprendo, la culpaba por ser la razón de la partida de mi padre.

Así pasaron meses. Un día mi madre trajó a la casa a cenar a un compañero de la oficina. Me habían advertido las dos que me portara bien. ¡En mi vida solamente tenía mujeres que me ordenaban y decían todo lo que debería hacer, desde mi madre y hermana a todas las maestras! También creo recordar que fue entonces cuando empecé a perder interés en todo lo que pasaba en el colegio. Dejé casi de tener amigos, y mis notas fueron bajando; no quise ni continuar jugando en el equipo de fútbol en el que llevaba muchos años. Para añadir más a mi tristeza, Charlotte empezó a salir con otro chico: David Epstein que siempre se reía de mí y me hacia burla cada vez que podía

Unas semanas antes de mi cumpleaños llegó, inesperadamente, un paquete de mi padre desde Alaska. En su interior había también una carta que no entendí muy bien ya que llevaba mucho tiempo sin hablar ni practicar el español. Mi padre me mandaba un precioso cuchillo esquimal y, según me dijo mucho después, me contaba la historia de cómo lo había conseguido. El simplemente tener en mis manos algo que mi padre había tenido en las suyas me llenó de alegría. Poco a poco, comencé a dominar la sensación de soledad que se había apoderado de mí.

Aquel verano mi madre se volvió a casar. Después de la boda, mi hermana y yo nos quedamos solos mientras ellos se fueron de viaje. Yo no me llevaba bien con mi hermana. Siempre había sentido que a la ruptura de mis padres ella había contribuido animando a mi madre y quejándose en todo momento de lo que hacía o decía mi padre. Una noche en que estaba solo en casa, se me ocurrió la brillante idea de llamar a mi padre por teléfono. No sabía su número y nunca le había llamado por conferencia; por eso me llevó bastante tiempo localizarle en la pequeña aldea en que vivía. Cuando oí su voz de nuevo me dio un vuelco el corazón. Le dije que me sentía muy triste sin él y, después de una corta conversación me preguntó si me gustaría ir a visitarle. Tardé mucho tiempo en poder encontrar a mi madre en el hotel en que estaban alojados durante su viaje de novios. La debí encontrar en un buen momento pues no opusó ninguna resistencia a que me fuera a Alaska.

El viaje fue largo y aburrido. No sé cuántas veces me dieron de comer en los distintos aviones pero lo cierto es que, al llegar, estaba completamente empachado y con mucho sueño. Mi padre y yo fuimos a pasar la noche a un hotelito en Anchorage antes de emprender la marcha a su nueva casa.

Lo primero que noté, al día siguiente, fue el frío espantoso que hacía y lo deprimente del cielo nublado. Aunque me había dicho que me trajera ropa de invierno, acostumbrado al clima caluroso del sur, el frío me molestó mucho. La aldea de mi padre estaba dentro de una reserva de indios esquimales. Mi primera sorpresa al llegar fue que una mujer nativa, creo que se llamaba

Keiko -o así me parece la llamaba mi padre- vivía en la casa. Mi padre hablaba con ella en su lengua nativa y, por mi parte, comprobé que su inglés era bastante limitado.

Mi padre y yo fuimos a pescar varias veces; poco a poco me fui acostumbrando al clima y al tipo de comida que era usual en aquella casa. Nunca me atreví a preguntar a mi padre por qué se había ido a vivir a aquel pueblo apartado de todo, entre gentes tan diferentes a él. Un día sin embargo, me di cuenta lo integrado que estaba dentro de la vida de la aldea. Ocurrió un accidente de avión a pocas millas de nuestra casa y mi padre se encargó de preparar el rescate que fue muy difícil pues el pequeño avión se había estrellado en lo más profundo de un valle rocoso.

Conociendo bien a mi padre, incluso a mi edad, pude notar una tristeza que trataba sin éxito de ocultar. Realmente no pude entender lo que hacía en la aldea, aunque muchos nativos le traían todo tipo de máquinas para arreglar; nunca le ví, sin embargo, recibir ningun dinero. Varias noches le vi sentado bebiendo whisky y le volví a ver en el mismo sitio por la mañana. Por lo que pude entender Keiko estaba preocupada por la cantidad de alcohol que consumía. También noté que en toda la casa no había un solo libro.

Quise hablar con él de cosas importantes; quería saber su opinión sobre la carrera que creía que debería estudiar en la universidad. Quería que me explicara por qué la vida es así; por qué no se pudó entender con mi madre; incluso me hubiera atrevido a preguntarle qué hacer con Charlotte antes que la perdiera completamente.

En el avión de regreso a casa, me di cuenta que tenía más preguntas que al comenzar mi viaje. Varios meses después me topé con unas cajas que contenían papeles de mi padre, y descubrí un diario que había escrito en su juventud. Mi español, para entonces se había deteriorado, por lo que decidí inscribirme en unos cursos por la noche. Entre aquellas clases y los papeles, artículos, y libros de mi padre fui poco a poco recuperando mi primera lengua. Tenía que controlar la cantidad y las veces que leía las cosas que él había dejado en aquellas cajas, pues siempre me entraba una gran tristeza. Vi cuentos, párrafos, poemas de gran belleza en que se notaba una gran sensibilidad y una mano mágica con las palabras.

Un día me llegó un telegrama de Keiko en que me informaba (yo había mantenido una correspondencia más o menos constante con los dos) que mi padre había muerto. Cuando conseguí hablar con ella por teléfono, comprendí que mi padre había puesto fin a su propia vida. Entre su inglés deficiente y su aversión a llamar las cosas por su nombre cuando, finalmente, tuve una idea clara de lo qué había pasado me sentía exhausto.

Al día siguiente me encontré, casualmente, con Charlotte. Advirtió inmediatamente qué me pasaba algo serio. Le conté, poco a poco, lo que había sucedido. Nunca había reflexionado sobre esto, pero me hubiera imaginado que ni siquiera recordaría a mi padre. Mi sorpresa fue total cuando sugeirió que fuéramos a las montañas donde íbamos de chicos con él. Allí pasamos todo el día recordándole, e incluso riéndonos de algunos incidentes que nos habían pasado.

Ahora en muchas ocasiones me voy yo solo a las montañas con algunas de las cosas que voy sacando de las cajas. Allí, en una soledad total, siento -mientras leo esas viejas páginas- que todavía estoy con mi padre. Si cierro los ojos me parece que podrá salir de entre los árboles en cualquier momento. Miro al solitario cielo azul; generalmente esa vitalidad de ese azul potente me vuelve a la vida. Hoy, sin embargo, recuerdo el frío que estará sintiendo en aquella congeladora soledad.

Roberto Pachecano

SAME-SAME

"Wait a minute! We're landing in a park in Danang, and people are barbecuing? What kind of war is this?" I shout to no one in particular. Only minutes ago the thought of arriving in war-torn Vietnam had worried me half-out of my mind—not the fear of going into battle but the lack of bullets for my M-14. What am I supposed to do? Throw my rifle at the Viet Cong and hope I score a direct hit . . . or use it to club'em to death?

We've been snookered, not by the Marine Corps but by the crew of the *USNS Walker*, a Merchant Marine troop carrier responsible for this "sissy" amphibious landing. Don't these contract sailors know that we just finished the most intensive training ever—Brainwashing 101? We were taught to fight and die for our country, or somebody's country, and these sea-going bellhops leave us at a picnic. I look out into the South China Sea as the *Walker's* crew stands along the deck laughing and waving at us. This surrealistic, city park port of entry fails to hint of war taking place, but we all know there is skirmishing on the other side of the smoking barbecue pits.

The hundred-odd Army soldiers accompanying the Marines on the three-week voyage from San Diego are not processed at the park but are herded into trucks to be transported elsewhere. Some of these guys are probably taking their last rides in a vehicle, realizing, like me, that they may soon be dressed in fashionable plastic and then stuffed into airtight tin-containers for the silent trip home.

The Marines fare no better. We're processing right then and

there in the park, next to picnic tables and smoking pits. What a fine how-do-you-do: coming 10,000 miles to die from smoke inhalation! Only a military mind could plan such a farce. We stand there coughing.

"PFC Pancho, front and center! Pancho! Pancho! Answer up, Asshole!" The redneck sergeant pauses briefly to spit out a mouthful of tobacco juice. "Where the fuck are you?"

The tanned, unshaven sergeant, about 30 years old, wears a flak jacket over a green, spit-splattered T-shirt. He walks with a noticeable limp which he attempts to disguise as a shuffling "ditty-bop" by swinging his "Devil-Dog" tattooed arm in a big arc from front to back. Helmet cocked on one side of his head, he looks as if he's swatting flies on his butt.

"Pancho!" the sergeant shouts. Pausing in front of each Marine, he looks at the name printed on the breast pocket of each utility shirt. Who the hell is this Pancho guy anyway? I grin as an image of Pancho Villa comes to me. I can almost hear him say, "What do you want, you dirty Gringo dog?"

I'll bet Pancho was the Marine who had the heart attack right before we landed at the park. What a way to go—didn't even get to hear the sound of gunfire. That thought is fleeting, however, as Sergeant Spittoon ditty-bops over to where I'm standing.

"There you are, you damned idiot," the sergeant shouts in my face. "Answer up when I call your name!" I almost gag at the smell of his breath. He must have eaten some of that Vietnamese barbecued meat. During our jungle warfare training at Camp Pendleton, California, an old-salt instructor told us that the Vietnamese were known to eat dogs. The sergeant's breath validated that story.

"You talking to me, Sarge?" I ask.

"Yeah, you, Pancho!" the sergeant barks. He spews pellets of spit past my face.

"My name isn't Pancho, Sarge!"

"Well, you're 'Pancho' to me. Get in line over there." He points to a small group of Marines lined up in front of the table next to the largest pit.

"My name isn't Pancho!" I shout. I ball my fists as I get ready to kick the shit out of this indignant peckerwood.

Spit starts to run down the side of the sergeant's mouth as his jaw drops slowly. He looks surprised as hell. He places the pen he's holding behind his ear, then brings his hand down to rest atop the .45 strapped to his waist. "Get over there, Marine!" he shouts. "I ain't going to tell you again!"

He calls me "Marine." The sergeant offers this as an apology while taking his big-ass foot out of the shit he has just stepped in. I spit on the ground and move toward the line.

I had lost my appetite two days out from Danang. The combination of rocking in a roiling sea and the thought of getting closer to the killing zone had made me too jittery to want food. Now I was getting hungry just standing in line and smelling the meat cooking in the pits. Funny. Who would've thought barbecued dog could make a taco bender's mouth water?

After a long wait in line, I finally reach a young Marine sitting on a box behind the processing table. He uses his bandaged left arm to hold down the pages of a name roster. My first thought is to ask him about his arm, but I decide against it because in the grand scheme of things, it doesn't matter.

"Name, rank and serial number!" The private never raises his head to look up at me.

I tell him. Then as an after-thought, I say, "and my name is not Pancho." The private grins and nods his head, still not looking up.

"You'll be assigned duty with Headquarters Company, 3rd Marines. That unit is here in Danang. Load your gear on Truck #4. God be with you. Next!" He continues to look down at the table. I almost expect him to genuflect as he sits there, head bowed. I don't want to read too much into this, so I gather up my gear and head toward the truck—a deuce-and-a-half. I climb in the back and join about eight other Marines.

Along the way to our unit, we pass a squalid village called "Dog Patch." Some Vietnamese stand in the doorways of dilapidated shanties, and some stand along the sides of the road. Some squat while straddling the sewer ditch to defecate. Only the newly-arrived Americans stare. Most of the shacks' windows are covered with bamboo shades while others are covered with cardboard. A few of the windows sport old, faded Coca-Cola signs—symbols of the more successful villagers. They all stare at Truck #4 as it belches diesel fumes from its exhaust pipe. These people all look alike— emaciated faces incapable of smiling. Camp Thien Shau, my new 'hood, sits on the side of a hill. In contrast to the village, named after a place only a cartoon character could call home, Thien Shau is an estate—manicured lawns in front of the officers' billets, white painted rocks delineating pathways, and generally a pristine-looking place, like American military bases back in the "world." The eight-hole outhouses at Thien Shau are modern marvels compared to the sewer ditches of Dogpatch.

I report to the 3rd Marines Command Post. After filling out necessary paperwork, Tom, the company clerk, takes four of us new guys to a vacant hootch on the other side of the hill near the road. Hootches are tent-like wooden huts with wire-meshed walls and tin roofs.

We are given the rest of the day to become familiar with the company's billeting area and to square away our quarters. After spending three weeks on the *Walker*, this hootch looks mighty good. I stumble while attempting to climb the three stairs leading into the hootch. I still have my sea-legs. As though floating on water, I make it through the hatch without any problems.

I set up my cot, unpack my duffel bag, and hang my combat gear and rifle on nails left there by the previous transients. I lie down to rest for a few minutes. The feeling of being in motion nauseates me somewhat, but I fall asleep anyway, just like a baby in a swinging cradle.

I don't know how long I slept when Marines yelling "Incoming!" and the sound of stampeding boots on the plywood floor shake me out of a catatonic state. Drooling and with eyes open as big as half-dollars, I get my ass up in a flash and run toward the hatch, following the dust trail left by assholes and belly-buttons, all headed into the bunkers located alongside the hootches.

Big mistake! I forget about my sea-legs. I run, half-leaning toward my right side, hit my shoulder on the corner of the hatchway, and spin as I exit. I completely miss the stairs and fall flat on my ass on the ground outside. In my current state of mind, coupled with my inability to run in a straight line, I crawl toward the bunker. This, too, becomes a problem as I try to avoid being stepped on by spooked stragglers. All the while, I hear screaming as Marines run by my crawling ass. No one offers me a hand.

I hear the laughter of children as I make my mad dash—mad crawl—to the bunker. Children? I've heard that people revert to their childhoods right before they die. "Shit!" Am I dying? I'm not wounded, so I'm convinced the laughter doesn't come from the mouths of children, but of angels. But then, how pretentious of me to even think that angels are coming for me when I die. "Sorry, God."

Once inside the bunker, we wait out the "red alert." A chorus of heavy breathing breaks the silence. My own thumping heartbeat resounds in my ears.

"False alarm," says one of the Marines in the bunker. "I hate this crap." He stands up, dusts himself off, and exits the hole I later call "purgatory."

I am the last one to step outside the bunker. As I walk back to my hootch, I look down the hill toward the road. Six young, Vietnamese boys stand there watching me, laughing. The angels. The boys, dressed in shirt-sleeves and short pants, are barefooted. All six of them wear Marine Corps utility caps, perhaps given to them by soft-hearted jarheads prior to their rotating back to the world.

One of the boys, the only one wearing a black shirt, brings his feet together, snaps to attention, and salutes me. I look around to see if anyone is looking, and I return his salute.

"Com eah, Moween!" says the kid who's probably the leader of the pack. I don't respond to his request. Instead, I think back to Camp Pendleton during my time with the staging battalion and remember being told not to trust any Vietnamese, especially the children, for fear they might be booby-trapped. "Com eah, ese!"

"Ese?" I am surprised by his calling me "Ese." This kid has been speaking to people from the Brown nation. In the barrio, "ese" means many things—guy, man, dude. I walk a little closer to the kid, then stop a few feet away.

"My nam Nguyen. You nam Vato!" the kid says and breaks into loud laughter.

I'm amused by this young boy, who looks to be about eight or nine years old. The other urchins seem to be about the same age as Nguyen.

"My nam Nguyen, you Vato!" he repeats.

I laugh. It's evident that some Chicano Marine has been this way before me. Nguyen starts rattling off all the words he knows in Spanish, as if engaged in a real "pachuco" conversation with me. He succeeds in his attempt to impress me. I hadn't had a good laugh since leaving LA, two weeks before boarding the *Walker*. I laugh again.

Back in LA, my buddies were "Red" Lyles from Detroit and "Bop City" Moorman from North Carolina, two black dudes I met at staging battalion in Camp Pendleton. Both "Red" and "Bop City" knew few phrases in Spanish—¿Que pasa? was one of them.

"¿Que pasa, Half-Breed?" they'd greet me, pleased with themselves. I told them hundreds of times that ¿Que pasa? was a Puerto Rican term and not a Chicano one. Chicanos, at least in my barrio, always said, ¿Que pasó? "Red" and "Bop City" didn't give a shit. They said I was half black and half white. It was okay. At least they didn't call me "Pancho." And I had a nick-name for them, too.

"You bunch of ignorant cotton-pickers," I'd say, each time they called me "Half-Breed."

"¡Piscadores Negros!" Lyles invariably retorted. "Black cotton-pickers!" We'd always laugh.

The last time I'd seen Lyles and Moorman was from the back of Truck #4 as it left the barbecue park. They were eating c-rations crouched in the shade beneath the tailgate of #8. They wave.

"¡Vayan con Dios, Amigos!" I shouted. "May God be with you!" Spanish is wasted on them.

Not so with Nguyen and his gang. They all try to learn by imitating him. These kids remind me so much of the kids in my barrio, Las Colonias, in San Antonio. The street was their playground. Always dirty and dusty from our dirt driveways, those kids, like these, shared muddy smudges on their faces. I start to get homesick. I stand there staring at the Vietnamese boys. Nguyen steps toward me.

"Hey, Vato? "Me, you, same-same?" Nguyen grins from ear to ear.

"What?" I don't understand what the kid is trying to tell me.

"You, me, same-same. Com eah," he said. He waves his hand in an up and down motion. It's like waving good-bye but at stomach level. "Com eah!" he says again, waving his hand, more pronounced this time.

I walk over and stand right next to him. I am not afraid of him anymore.

"Same-same!" he keeps saying again and again, touching me on the arm, then touching his arm, then mine, then his.

I get it! Nguyen is trying to tell me that he and I share the same skin color—brown. So I say, "Same-Same!" I touch his arm, then mine.

"Ya! Me, you, vatos, same-same, brudders!"

"Yes, Nguyen. We same-same, vatos, brothers!"

Nguyen grabs my hand and attempts to pull me toward the road. I balk.

"No, Nguyen. No can do. No can go across road. Captain say no," I claim. I feel like an idiot talking like Tarzan. But I don't know how else to say it. I feel like I'm making fun of the way Nguyen talks. Nguyen doesn't care.

"You com my home, Vato. Mudder. Brudders. You eat. They same-same you. They like." Nguyen continues to pull on my hand. "They same-same you, Vato."

I like this kid. There is a war going on and he invites me to his home for dinner. But what Nguyen doesn't know is that I wouldn't go to his place for all the money in the world. No sir. Brainwashing

101 is too fresh.

"No, Nguyen. No can go. You stay here." Nguyen squats down on his haunches and waits by the bunker. I go into my hootch and return with a couple of cans of C-rations—lima beans. I open a can and show it to Nguyen.

"NO, VATO!" Nguyen jumps back as if I were holding a snake in my hand. "Number ten! No good. You eat number ten!" He covers his mouth with both hands. We both start laughing. I can't understand why everyone seems to hate lima beans. I love them, especially with jalapeno peppers. Since I don't have any peppers, I bring out a bottle of Tabasco sauce, just in case. But with Nguyen's protest weighing heavily on me, I go back in and get three cans of beef and potatoes. We sit on the ground side by side and share the military meal. He eats from the can in front of him, his other arm hugs me tight around my back. We each eat a can of rations.

"¡Oralé, Vato. Eso!" Nguyen says. I laugh. I'm amazed that Nguyen knows the meaning of eso (way to go). He never stops surprising me. "Vato, you no want?" Nguyen points to the remaining can.

"No, Vato. You eat."

With that, Nguyen picks up the can and runs toward the rice paddy across the road about a hundred yards away. At one point he stops running and hops on one leg as he retrieves the rubber sandal he lost as his foot hit the berm. We laugh. Nguyen runs up to an old man who squats at the edge of the paddy. The old Vietnamese tends his grazing water buffalo. Nguyen gives the old man the can of beef and potatoes. The kid turns around and points toward me. The man tips his straw hat and waves only once. Nguyen runs back and sits next to me again. He continues to hug me. We sit looking at the old man as he finishes his food, puts the empty can in a burlap sack that hangs from his side, and slowly walks away with his buffalo lumbering behind him.

"You number one, Nguyen." I hold my index finger up.

"No, Vato. You number one." Nguyen holds his finger high overhead as if pointing to the sky.

In the short time since meeting Nguyen, I've been able to relax more, and the war jitters have settled down. The kid would do well in my barrio.

I see my vato-brudder ten, fifteen more times during the coming month. Each time I give him a small gift—candy, c-rations, a few MPC—war dollars. To Nguyen, however, these gifts are treasures. They represent love and friendship, something far different from the war he's always known in his young life. He thanks me with a hug. And he always holds his index finger high above his head and says, "You, number one!" It's a ritual.

"You, me, vatos, brudders. Same-Same!" Nguyen never fails to greet me the same way every time. A couple of my hootch-mates liked to rib me each time they see me talking to the kid. "He's pulling the wool over your eyes, Pancho," or "That kid is gonna kill you some day."

I usually ignore the prophecies, but it's difficult. Could they possibly be right? I hope not. I think about the bubba-sergeant on my first day in 'Nam, the one who called me Pancho. That "numbnuts" turned out to be a prophet.

The Anglo Marines, now joined by the Blacks, call me Pancho. Kicking ass and getting kicked doesn't dissuade anyone from calling me the dreadful name given to most Chicanos. It is, however, a lot better than being called Chico, like many other Chicanos are tagged. I give up trying to stop Marines from calling me Pancho, but I don't give up on Nguyen. Me and Nguyen are brudders—same-same. The kid's presence gives me the feeling of having family around. The others should be so lucky, but leave it to the Marine Corps to screw things up.

Someone at headquarters decided Vietnamese are no longer welcome near our hootches. Navy Seabees put up a fence on the berm, next to the rice paddy closest to the dirt road. This is about a hundred to a hundred and fifty meters away. The area is now off-limits to Vietnamese. If caught inside the new perimeter, they will be detained. I see Nguyen a few more times as he stands by the fence saluting me. He points to his arm. I salute back. I point to my arm.

"Same-same," I muse. I never see Nguyen again.

I have been in country fewer than ninety days, when Tom, the clerk, tells me I'm being re-assigned to the 9th Marine Regiment. "They're moving to the DMZ in two days. Pack your gear and Hasta la Vista, Pancho."

"Wait a minute, Tom. How did I get this primo transfer?"

"Captain Jones pulled your name out of his helmet. He said you'd be okay with it, since you been bugging him to send you out to a rifle company." Tom shrugs his shoulders as he leans closer to me and asks, "But at the DMZ?"

"Don't worry, Tom. I'm ready. Hoorah!"

Two days later I'm at Dong Ha with the "Striking 9th." I should have taken the lightning bolt over the 9 on the unit's logo as a hint of things to come. Dong Ha is nothing more than a large hill of red dirt. For a second, I thought I was back in South Texas. I begin to feel a little homesick. But the feeling lasts only a few seconds as the chop-chop sound of helicopter blades breaks the moisture-laden air and quickly jolts me back to reality.

Me and four other Marines are given a ten-man canvas tent. We're told to pitch our new dream house next to the tin-roofed hootches with walls of screen mesh. I guess the screen mesh is for keeping the gook 'squitos out.

As in Danang, the hootches are separated with bunkers, holes in the ground piled high with sandbags. The next hint is a visual—there are many holes in the sandbags. Shrapnel. After we pitch the tent, we get busy filling sandbags and lining them up four feet high along the tent's perimeter—nice and close to the heads of our cots. We roll the sides of the tent up, high enough to let some hot air in. Hot air was invented in 'Nam, I think.

We finish stacking the sandbags. I lie down on my cot for a minute, just long enough for the hot air to blow on my sweaty fatigues, and cooling me down a few degrees. I say to myself, "Now this is a dream house."

Kaboom! Whump! Kaboom! Whump! My cot breaks as I push down hard on the wooden frame. I jump out of it and head toward the bunker, now endlessly far away. Outside, I almost run into another Marine who's dug his boots into the dirt, extending his arms out in front of him to brace himself for the impact. "Whoa! They're our guns," he says. "It's the 12th Marines, an artillery unit, on the next hill. The shells are 'outgoing', Stupid!"

Tonight would be the first of many sleepless nights. I never get used to the explosions—the real ones and the louder ones in my nightmares.

About a month later I am walking across the regimental compound, I come upon a dozen or so enemy POW's guarded by a few Marines. Some of them wear black pajama-type clothing; others wear remnants of NVA uniforms. Most of the dinks are blind-folded. The ones that aren't stare at me as I walk by. My steps begin to slow. The dinks have a sad, pathetic, far-away look in their deep sunken eyes, made more pronounced by their high, protruding cheek-bones. The prisoners look emaciated. Each has his hands tied together, and all are tied to each other.

The sight of them standing there in silence gives me an eerie feeling. I hear no sound. I see no emotion. I imagine dead dinks as I stop and let my M-14 slide down my shoulder and into my sweating hands. I feel the anger stirring the butterflies inside my gut. I think of how much I have come to hate the gooks. I want to blow them away.

"Keep moving, Marine!" one of the guards calls out to me.

The guard's loud, hoarse voice snaps me out of my trance. I sweat as I slowly walk away. *"Lord, why am I so angry? What have these Vietnamese done to me? Please help me. I don't know what to do,"* I pray under my breath as I clear the area and return to my tent.

I'm in my "dream house." Nguyen enters my thoughts. I wonder what he's doing. I'll bet a hundred dollars he's saluting some Chicano right about now. I smile. Or maybe he's dead. All bets are off. My smile vanishes.

I think of Nguyen's friends in Danang, the rest of the Vietnamese vatos whom I had befriended earlier in the year. I remember their dirty, smiling faces. Their biggest smiles flashed when I gave them the tortillas my mom always sent me in her care-packages. The boys had eaten them before, thanks to another good-hearted Pancho. Like me, other brown Marines also felt these vatitos were "same-same" as the kids in the barrio—our brothers and sisters. If they only knew.

Night comes. I can't rest, much less sleep, most of the time. I lie on my cot thinking of the POW's I saw earlier in the day. I wonder if they miss their families as much as I do mine. Nah. How could they miss their families? These guys with the blank stares . . . the ones without emotion . . . the silent ones. The ones who hide behind blind-folds. I feel sorry for them. I can't help it. They are "same-same" me.

The heat under the canopy of the canvas tent is unbearable. I am sweat-drenched. I can hardly breathe. I lie there listening to an occasional shell bursting somewhere on something or some-one. "Tat-tat-tat-tat," the sound of a Marine's automatic weapon fired in the distance, mixes with the cacophony of chirping night-critters and the drum-roll sound of rat feet running along the sandbags next to my head.

My thoughts of Nguyen, his vatito buddies, the POW's—the "Gooks"— reveal something to me. Never during my entire tour of duty in Vietnam did any Marine, any fellow American, military or civilian, ever declare himself the same as me. Never! Nguyen, the Vietnamese-vato, was not only telling me we shared the same skin color. He was telling me in broken Vietnamese-English-Span-ish that we were both God's children—"Same-Same."

Beth Rodriguez

NO HABLO ESPAÑOL

I can't speak Spanish. No hablo español.

In my fantasy world, I'm fluent. I speak effortlessly, with ñ's and ll's rolling easily off my tongue. No grasping for words—my thoughts move seamlessly from English to Spanish as the conversation flows from one subject to another.

Real life is somewhat different.

The situation usually goes something like this:

I'm introduced to a native Spanish-speaker, who immediately notes my very Latino surname.

"Rodriguez?" He or she pauses for a beat, and I brace for the question I know is coming. "Do you speak Spanish?"

"A little," I hedge.

Upon which a torrent of questions en castellano are released upon me. I struggle under the onslaught. My thought processes slow and my tongue grows large and unwieldy in my mouth. What's the past imperfect of that verb? Do I use a direct or indirect object? As any knowledge I have of the language slowly seeps out of my brain, my cheeks flush. After I force out a few halting sentences, my inquisitor usually takes pity on me and changes the subject.

So why can't I speak Spanish? Or, more to the point, why can't I speak Spanish *well*?

The answer requires a brief family history. My father, born and raised in Peru, came to the U.S. to go to college. He met and married my mother, the daughter of Swedish immigrants. After a few years, I was born. They decided to speak to me in both

English and Spanish, so I would grow up bilingual. (My mother learned Spanish after meeting my father.)

By the age of two, my vocabulary consisted of "Mom", "Dad", and "No." My mother was afraid I wasn't going to talk at all, so they switched to just speaking to me in English.

I don't know if they regret that decision, but I certainly have. There are few things more frustrating to a child than standing in a room full of relatives and not being able to understand a word being said.

Sometimes frustration became painful. Like when mi abuelo became sick. I remember our last visit to Peru before he died. Like my parents, I wanted to tell him I was worried about him not eating, that I wanted him to get better and I loved him. But I had to wait for my parents to translate, or smile and squeeze his hand and hope that could communicate enough.

Not that I was completely Spanish-illiterate growing up. I said my prayers in Spanish (although to be honest, I wasn't usually sure exactly what I was praying for), could sing "Feliz Cumpleaños" and knew basic phrases.

My parents enrolled me in extracurricular "conversational Spanish classes" when I was in elementary school, which would help...for a while. I would dutifully do my assignments and practice with my parents, and my Spanish would improve. But the class would end, and I'd slip back into just speaking in English.

The same scenario more or less repeated itself in high school and college courses. Don't get me wrong, my knowledge and understanding of the language did improve. Depending on the accent of the speaker and the complexity of the topic, I could usually understand what was being said. And I would occasionally renew my efforts to speak Spanish at home, but more than a decade of habit would work against me.

No hablo español

It wasn't only habit that made my Spanish-speaking efforts short-lived, however.

I knew that I was an intelligent young woman. Speaking in English, I was relatively articulate and had a fairly large vocabulary to work with. But trying to express myself in Spanish was like trying to speak with a gag on. I knew what I wanted to say, but I couldn't get the words out.

It's hard to discuss the surrealism of Lorca's poetry or the characterization of women in Pedro Almodovar's films using the vocabulary of a child. And it's embarrassing to be acutely aware of the seconds ticking by as one scours her brain for the correct word, inwardly wincing at her own halting, error-filled speech. With each mistake, I grow more anxious, and any knowledge of the language flees to the farthest corners of my brain.

Get over it, was the simple but very valuable advice I received in the spring of my junior year in college. In my quest to learn Spanish, I spent a semester in Cordoba, Spain and explained my predicament to a local friend. She reassured me that my Spanish was "fine", but more importantly, she pointed out that I was judging myself harder than anyone else was.

I was never going to be able to speak Spanish well if I didn't speak it at all. That is, if I kept my mouth shut for fear of making a mistake. People would be understanding if my grammar was somewhat mixed-up or my speech a little slow.

The logical part of me knows this is true, but it's still hard to keep from feeling self-conscious. No matter how patient the conversation partner, it's uncomfortable to feel you are holding up the discussion. Interestingly, I'm more at ease when the person I am speaking with doesn't know English, perhaps because I feel more in control of the situation.

So why do I care if I'm fluent or not? It's not as if my situation is unique. There are hundreds of second-, third- and fourth-generation Latinos and Latinas in the U.S. who aren't bilingual, for one reason or another.

I don't need Spanish in my day-to-day life. I don't live in an area of the country with a sizeable Latino population, and in the rare occasions where a knowledge of Spanish is relevant, I usually know enough to get by, even if I'm sometimes awkward socially.

Still, I yearn to hablar español como una nativa. To read a short story by Ana María Matute without a Spanish-English dictionary by my side. To watch a Mexican film without having to sneak an occasional glance at the subtitles.

To speak the language of my father and grandparents. As I learned in linguistics, language is the bearer of culture. It codifies the unique experiences and traditions of a civilization, which is why some words just can't be translated. I want that link, that shared culture, with a family and people thousands of miles away from me. A heritage to be shared with my own children (God help them, if I have any) when the time comes, one that encompasses everything from churros to los Reyes Magos.

I can't speak Spanish the way I want to. Not yet. But I keep my dictionary beside me and try to remember that it's not how well I speak that matters, but simply that I speak.

Maria Elena Perez

THE MANY LANGUAGES I SPEAK

In my freshman year at college, I came across essays written by Amy Tan and Gloria Anzaldúa about the many languages we speak. It prompted me to think about the many languages I spoke. Here is a short, and by all means, an incomplete list: "standard" English, "standard" Spanish, slang English, *cibaeño* Dominican Spanish, Puerto Rican Spanish, and Spanglish. And this list does not take into account the different accents my tongue at times speaks English in, including Dominican, Puerto Rican, Brooklyn, and New York. Like many Latino bilingual students in public city schools, the language spoken at home is far different from the one spoken in school, which is also different from the one spoken on the streets. In my case, the language spoken at home, Spanish, was completely different from the one spoken in school, English. In addition, there were different "Spanishes" and "Englishes" I spoke. Growing up in a largely Latino community in Brooklyn, New York I learned to switch back and forth between all these languages. Language switching became a mode of survival in different contexts.

My first language is Spanish, however, my dominant language is English. I am orally and verbally fluent in both, however, I have noticed that my Spanish emotional vocabulary does not rival that of my English emotional vocabulary. I realized my mild Spanish impotence as a social work intern. It is hard to sit with a client and try to help them access their emotional realm, when I cannot do the same in Spanish. Growing up, speaking about my feelings or my emotions was not something I did with Spanish speaking family or friends. With friends, that is what I had English for. I developed most of my emotional thought and accessed these feelings in English, mainly with friends and boyfriends. My emotional Spanish vocabulary was trapped – in poems and essays that allowed me to access this world. This world is private, it never engaged with others. Now, I am learning to engage in this manner, in Spanish, right alongside my clients. This is just one example of the many times I have realized the power and sometimes impotence of language use.

I also noticed the impotence of language when I accompanied my mother and family friends to social service agencies when I was a child. Their one language dominance proved to be impotent in the dominant English speaking agencies. It was on these diligencias, or errands, that I felt my mother and her friends' impotence, and I, on the other hand, felt empowered and saddened because of my command of two languages. It saddened me because I realized that this power was dependent on someone else's powerlessness – my mother's. The realization of this dichotomy when applied to life in general still saddens me.

And my language inventory is not limited to just English and Spanish. Growing up and even to this day, I use different languages within different contexts to "fit in." When I am around old Brooklyn friends, I will use some good ol' Brooklyn English slang. With my Dominican friends, I whip out the Dominican Spanglish. At home, I speak purely Spanish and often throw in some English words and phrases that my mom has come to understand like "corny," "nasty," and "I don't care." At work and with college friends, I speak English. Sometimes this English is more formal and other times it's relaxed, a mix of formal and Brooklyn English. What I have come to understand from all my uses of English is that my language potential is maximized in this language. I unleash its full verbal potential.

With old around the way Brooklyn friends, my English is diluted. It is constrained. It is limited. The most powerful reason for not using "standard English" with these old friends is that one runs the risk of being called "White" or thought of as "a sell out," better than everyone else, where "everyone else" is really just them, your old friends. What ends up occurring is that Standard English use is equated with class, status, and as impersonating the dominant socio-economic class – the Whites. For Blacks, you run the risk of being called an "Oreo" and for Asians you run the risk of being called a "banana." As human beings, we fear rejection and want to be accepted, and as the child of immigrant parents, this was no different. I wanted to be accepted by my peers, both the ones on my block and the ones at school. These feelings persisted until I began college.

It wasn't until college that I realized another one of language's powerful uses, that of division. I knew growing up that if I spoke a certain way, other than the norm in that given context, that I would run the risk of excluding my audience from what I wished to communicate. However, after college I discovered that even though I wished to speak with these old friends, I sometimes did not receive any fulfillment from the conversation. Sure, one often runs into old friends or desires to see them and the purpose of the language then is to catch up and to remember old times, and that is fine. What is not fine, to me, was when I tried to keep old friendships where the present conversations were not meaningful, where the language divided us. My English wanted to run free and express all the new thoughts and views I have taken, but using my old English was like going back to that old self. In these instances, not only did my language use serve as a division between my old friends and I, it also served as a division and marker between my old and forming new identities.

Another way that I have noticed the power of language in my own life, as a bilingual Latina, is the use and preference of Spanish or English when speaking with other bilingual Latinas. Usually when speaking about issues related to sex and sexuality, we would use English. Most of my Latina friends came from traditional and often religious, Spanish-speaking only, Dominican or Puerto Rican families where sex was not discussed. This meant that we spoke of such matters amongst ourselves in English so that our parents would not understand – another form of lingual divide. In addition, it shaped our sexual attitudes and experiences within an English, American context and subsequently our sexual identities evolved as a function of what we identified as our American identities. We led double lives, one in Spanish at home and one in English at school and with friends. We were the little *virgencitas* at home and outside of our homes, we were as Americans call it, *coming of age*.

All these experiences led me to two conclusions – not only have my languages shaped my experience of life, but also that my experience of life has shaped my languages. And it continues to have this reciprocal relationship. There is a bit of me in all the languages I speak, some bits bigger than others, but nonetheless present and a reminder of where I came from and where I am now. Not so deep within me is the "improper" English speaking, with a Brooklyn accent girl that serves as a memory of childhood and adolescence. And this girl exists within the educated, standard English speaking, but sometimes with a Spanish accent, woman that she's become. A woman that considers herself bilingual in the technical sense, but multilingual in the context of her life. Now I pose you the question, what languages do you speak?

Toni Nelson Herrera

BREATHING IN SPANISH

Back when this project was just an idea I told my grandmother Alicia and her younger brother, my great uncle Eddie (who is closer in age to my own mother than his older sister), about it. It was the first time they'd told me in such detail, and as an adult, about what their young lives were like in Crystal City, Texas in the thirties and forties—a town which later became famous for its role in the Chicana/o movement. In certain circles, especially in political ones, just mentioning the name of this town causes ears to perk up, heads to turn, people to ask questions, and of course make assumptions. Having trained as a historian I wanted to know directly what the social fabric of life in Cristál, as the residents call it, was like. My uncle summed it up simply, "You couldn't even breathe in Spanish."

snapshots

When I think of history—big "H" History—I can't always think of how to express certain things that are so important, it seems to me, to say. I guess I feel the same way about literature, these words are so big and intimidating, and despite all my years of study seem ever elusive and a bit out of reach. It's like words are such a failing—they don't quite capture experience. Or maybe I'm just a failure with words. Sometimes I'll paint or make sculptures or draw instead, and then I'll write. I mix it all up in a swirl of expression because nothing I do seems to come out the way I want it to. I just know that some serious things have happened that I can't put down in any way that holds my life experiences still long enough for me to get a handle on them. The memories keep slipping away into shadows as time wears on so I just want to hold them here like small, carved out sculptures of lives I've known, for one more look, for a chance to call them history/historia or art/arte—words I don't understand.

hands
My great-grandmother had long, neatly braided gray and black hair trailing down her back and she leaned forward at the shoulders. She was less than five feet tall, and had an amazing presence. I loved the way, I remember, that she always greeted me-like it was pure joy to see me or any of the grandchildren or great grandchildren she had.

Every time I saw her she would envelop my face with her hands. I was impressed by the way they were deeply wrinkled on the backs with very smooth palms. Her large hands almost seemed too big for her small size. She would pat my cheeks gently and look deeply into my eyes and then back and forth to my mother seeming to offer approving words. Maybe she was just noticing how much I looked like my aunts and my mother. It was amazing to me, even as a little girl, to be from such a long line of women and I looked at all of them wondering what my life would be like.

On a vacation to Crystal City that my family made from southern California my brothers and I were left with my great grandmother while my parents ran errands. I was unsure about being left alone with her because my mother emphasized that she spoke only Spanish and I realized, in the way things become clearer to you as a child, that I spoke only English.

I wasn't sure what to do, but trusted that my parents must know what they were doing—the way you have to as a child when they leave you. My great grandmother didn't seem worried either, and started to speak to me anyway. I looked up at her sweet face, with its deeply carved lines like rivers through a sandy desert, and somehow understood what she was saying. It seemed strange to me, all this awareness and concern, and yet everything was fine. I could understand her. It was like magic, if you don't think about it too hard it works perfectly well, but if you do it spoils it.

niña

One summer after we'd gotten back from Texas my mom and my brothers and I met up with my father in San Luis Obispo—this was the mid-seventies. He was no longer working at the Purina (dog food) factory in Fontana, but was in college that summer. We went to the grocery store to buy food and I remember seeing a children's picture book that was in Spanish and wanting to have it.

Usually we didn't ask for things because we knew our parents didn't have money, but I wanted it so badly that I asked anyway just in case. My parents bought me the thin paper book along with the groceries. It was the only book I ever had as a child that was my own. My brothers and I had only a couple of books and a few of the letters of the alphabet from a children's encyclopedia series between us that, like everything, we shared.

I read the book over and over and learned the words like niña and perro and lapiz. I thought it seemed like a lot of extra work that the words ended in a's for girls and o's for boys, but the words seemed so beautiful to me. I liked how colorfully the book was drawn, and the way the people in it looked, and getting to see the words matched up with the objects they described. I was always asking questions about my mother's family and about life in Texas, and getting her to explain the few family photos and the people and places in them. One time my mom told me my first words were in Spanish.

I couldn't remember my first words, though I would guess they were probably papas because she always told me to "eat my papas." I did remember not wanting to use a fork, that was way too much trouble for me. I preferred using a rolled tortilla instead and held out as long as I could from using a fork, using my hands and my tortillas to eat lengua.

waiting

One of the biggest influences of my life in terms of language was my father who was not Mexican American, but Anglo. He was my mother's second husband, they met while she was pregnant with me and he married her after I was born. He was the only father I ever had or wanted to have. My father took the idea of "marrying into the family" very seriously. He learned Spanish in order to be able to communicate with my grandmother and my great grandmother, and would either write or speak to them over the phone in Spanish. They adored him because of this.

Because of this example, I also tried to write my great grandmother, but no one told me before I started that she could not read very well. I did not know how to write in Spanish either so I lay on the living room floor on my belly with a dictionary at my side, while my parents sat talking, and wrote a letter to her in English. Then I painstakingly "translated" it into Spanish word for word. It wasn't until I studied Spanish years later that I realized that my "translation" couldn't possibly have made any sense. Knowing my great grandmother though, she probably just saved the letter along with all the other regalitos people gave her that she kept on display in her tiny home along with her handmade flowers and crochet work.

In California where I grew up we lived out in the country, and my father worked with students and their farm projects. I would often drive with him in his work truck down the country roads on the way to see other people's farms and visit their animals to check on their health. He would try to teach me Spanish by naming things that he saw along the way, conejos, arboles, piedras. His routine efforts increased my vocabulary and made it fun to learn.

It seems like I was always trying to learn Spanish. My mother would hold me in her lap, I remember, and sing to me, "tengo la muñeca vestida azul, con su zapatitos y su camisol" which sounded like one long word to me so I would make her slow down and touch her lips with fingers so I could stop her and ask what each word meant. As the years went on she spoke Spanish less and less, though the racism she endured because of her brown skin never let up.

The years went by, and after he'd had his third surgery for a tumor that persistently grew into his brain I went to see my father in the hospital. It was the last time I ever saw him lucid. As I was walking around the curtain to see him, he was sitting up in bed, awake. He was silent, and I wasn't sure, given the surgery, if he could even speak anymore, much less recognize me. But he did. He spoke to me in Spanish. I couldn't believe it. Here he'd had a terrible seizure, and subsequent brain surgery, and here he was speaking to me in his non-native language. I couldn't believe he even remembered that I was taking Spanish in High School, the one he'd taught at until this time.

No language could express the loss of my father, and my "family", as a result of this death. Not long after he died, my great-grandmother died too. She later appeared to me in a dream, but didn't speak to me, just held my face in her hands for one last look and then disappeared down a long, winding path into the distance. I wanted to go with her, but it wasn't my time yet. How many roads can we stumble down in our grief? How many roads to nowhere are there?

more waiting

Somehow I continued on in High School during those dying years, and I kept trying to learn Spanish too. I signed up for Spanish 1 twice, and Spanish 2 once, but I could never speak the way I wanted to. I remember trying to learn to tell time in Spanish. I couldn't tell time in English either, but this was right around the time that digital clocks started to be mass produced so I figured I could just get by. My teachers always told me I had great pronunciation skills, and I did well on my tests, but I was still sad that I didn't really know it. I'd been trying to learn it for years, but between my little paper book and my overcrowded public school classes it just wasn't happening.

I would ask my mother why she didn't teach us Spanish. I told her how much easier it would have been if she'd taught it to me, but she didn't seem to have the words herself for why this was the case. It was like we didn't even know who we were in the world. You didn't see people that looked like us on t.v., and were hardly talked about in the English media. I was going to school with a white majority, and myself and the other Mexican American kids (I called myself Mexican American back then) just looked quietly at each other.

In southern California if you were light brown and could speak good unaccented English it was like you just had a "good tan." I was always praised by white kids for my incredible tanning abilities. My brothers and my mother on the other hand were often terribly mistreated for their darker skin tones, from physical assault, to being pulled over by cops, to being tracked into lower level classes at school (even being put into what they used to call "retarded" classes), to being abused by bosses, to not being hired, to always being talked to like they were stupid, to not being allowed in certain parts of town, no matter how clear and unaccented their speech was they were always reminded of the meaning of their skin. If I ever insisted to white kids that I was Mexican American they would retort, "you're not like the other Mexicans, we like you!" as if they were somehow complimenting me.

None of this made sense to me until I went to college and started taking U.S. History classes and putting the pieces of the puzzle of this language/political past together by taking first African American History, and then Chicana/o History. I was so angry every day of college. The shock of growing up disadvantaged and deeply alienated reverberated through my brain with every book I read. I only missed a single lecture in those years, and even then I got the notes and got my roommate to tell me every word she could remember. I couldn't take one more day of lies, and I didn't want to miss my chance to learn more because I recognized my education as my only tool for self-defense in this world. I bought all the books they assigned, and kept all of them except those I gave away to my mother because she'd always wanted an education—that is what had driven me over all the obstacles in my path—that sense of fulfilling her life's dreams.

After studying Chicana/o History I could place my family historically. I could understand what it meant to have had an Anglo father raise me. With history I could understand and place the racism of my mother's first husband's Jewish family that had contributed to him abandoning her and leaving my mother with two kids and no education and no hope for a future. But there were things that education couldn't tell me, things that I now became empowered to theorize from own experiences. I tried to explain to the racist students in my graduate classes why we read historical literature by Chicanas when they said they shouldn't have to read it because the writing was so bad in their eyes. I tried to explain to my racist professors, who get to stand as the gatekeepers of history, why I wanted to study what I do, and be the kind of professor I want to be despite what they say against me.

more waiting

The money that helped me to go to college came from my father's teachers retirement benefits. Because he didn't live long enough to retire my brothers and I were legally entitled to some money towards helping us, but only if we enrolled in school. I was the only one who managed to hold myself together so soon after this death to be able to take advantage of this opportunity—I knew it was my only chance to go to college and I was terrified to lose it in every sense of the word.

My mother would send me a check for $500 every month from the Teacher's Retirement System, and I worked part-time jobs and earned another $400 dollars a month; from this I paid my tuition and bills and saved money by wearing old clothes, never cutting my hair, and skipping meals. Twice I spent my savings from this income, everything I had, on learning Spanish. The first time for Summer Language intensive class that finally got me speaking and even dreaming in Spanish. Later I saved to be able to go to Mexico after I graduated from college without having to ask anyone for help. I was always broke, and on a budget. I budgeted all the way down to the two quarters per laundry load to be able to go see what Mexico was really like instead of what the dominant white society in the U.S. had been telling me all my life.

I tried and tried to learn Spanish with what little means I've had my whole life. In political settings though it never mattered who I was, our history, how I'd tried can so easily be brushed aside in a moment I found. Language experiences in our communities differ so much, and we have such a strong legacy of self hate. It doesn't surprise me anymore to not be understood, doesn't slow me down. I know what my commitments are, and I know that there is a place for people with similar experiences within Chicana/o history, and I know by teaching it I will keep that space open for as long as it's needed.

getting there

In political settings when we break the silence I know that there are plenty of other Chicana/os like me who aren't fluent, but exist in multiple spaces, and do political work anyway. I know someone will make a crack about not speaking Spanish, or assume we all do, but I'm empowered enough to speak for myself. You can't let yourself be tied up in waiting for understanding, expecting others to "get you" because they won't, but they may meet you part way and for that I can be grateful. Whether I become another Chicana professor wading through the battles over "authenticity", I know the history that made someone like me possible and that can never be taken away from me. I also know my part in creating the hope that there could be a different, more helpful outcome than our past would imagine.

one more breath

These words are dedicated to the memories of my antepasados who weren't able to breathe the way they wanted to, and had no chance at the kinds of educational opportunities that I have had, as painful as they have been. All of these memories are my pieces of history, my words on paper, my say about what has happened, my say about what it means to be me and to also be a part of them. I have been trying for so long to have my say—please don't let anyone stop you until you've had yours.

Louis G. Mendoza

LENGUA AMERICANA, CORAZÓN CHICANO: FINDING MY VOICE

Compulsory monolingualism strips people of their natural voice— to sing, to shout, to express love and rage in their native tongue. My story is one about the secondary effects of racial violence caused by institutional racism and social prejudice, forces that rob people not only of their native language but their authentic voice. My story may not be a story about the loss of a particular language (can one lose what one never had?) as much as it is about my quest to regain my voice so I could use it—as an art form, a weapon, and a bridge to understanding.

Somewhere in my childhood, understanding and love tran- scended language—or at least my understanding and experience of love was not limited to language. When I was a child our large family's Sunday visits to our maternal and paternal grandparents were as regular as church. We tumbled out of the station wagon and paid homage to our grandparents, whose small houses smelt like the inside of a cedar chest and were as neat and clean as they were dark and cool. The visits always started off formally with a ritual hug, kiss, and pinch of the cheek followed by a sur- vey of our appearance. We kids marveled at how these small two bedroom wood-frame houses had managed to hold our parents' larger families of six and nine children respectively. Invariably, after our grandparents asked us how school was going in their halting English, the conversation between grandma and grandpa and mom and dad would take place almost exclusively in Span- ish. Sometimes we stayed listening in amazement at how they could understand each other when it seemed everyone was talking as fast as they could all at the same time. You didn't hear that kind of simultaneous exchange among English speakers. Why was it that the English in our house required that only one person at a time speak? Usually we drifted off and wandered outside to play in the yard or sit on the porch. Sometimes one or more of us stayed around and let the conversation wash over us like a cool summer breeze hypnotizing us with its rich cadence and often lulling us to sleep because, in truth, though there was something nice about witnessing the exchange of familial intimacies and intricacies of life between the generations, we understood almost nothing being said.

Grandma and grandpa on both sides of the family spoke little English despite having lived in Texas the vast majority of their lives. Driven from their home country by the Mexican Revolution and lured here by promises of economic opportunity, they each arrived separately in Texas sometime between 1911 and 1915. Fifty and sixty years later they could look back upon their lives of work, of survival, of hardship, of tenacity, and yes, of dignity and progress despite an often unwelcome social and political climate. Though I know they loved us, their children's children, dearly, our relationship was mitigated by our mutual language limits. Separated from them by only a generation our first language was English. So it was that we moved among them with respect, a respect not unlike our Catholicism, borne of fear and love—undergirded by these qualities, our relationship was also limited by our ignorance of the particulars of their lives.

Years later I would wonder how they felt about this generational shift, this language gap that existed between us. Did they think us sell-outs, cultural misfits, as a tragic consequence of assimilation, or did they foresee that cultural characteristics like language would be the price we paid for "Americanization," for "progress"? From my perspective as a child, I saw them as a link to an archaic past, one that I did not fully understand yet nevertheless knew I should revere. And despite not being able to share the details of our lives with them, I sensed that we pleased them, and that they loved us unconditionally despite our language differences. One of my earliest memories as a child is of Grandma Martinez. I recall hiding behind her skirts when my parents came to pick me up after they had been on a trip. I clung to her because I was mad and hurt at having been left behind. In her firm, but gentle and loving way, she reconnected me with my parents. I also have early memories of playing underneath the banana trees on the side of their house; it was a place that, along with the magnolia trees, provided cool shade in the heat of the summer. I recall spending weekends at grandma and grandpa Mendoza's house with my cousin Jesse. We played and always obeyed their commands to do this or that chore, and we always felt safe.

I can't help but believe that in my pre-school years I was at least partly bilingual. I don't recall having any communication problems with my grandparents during these visits, even when I occasionally spent several consecutive days there. Our presence, whether as adults or as children mostly interested in playing, always seemed to matter to them—we never felt lost in the sea of grandchildren, not even when we had those huge Christmas reunions that made me feel like we could start our own neighborhood. Our grandparents were the calm in the storm of all that joyful craziness—they emanated grace and soothing love—and in this way our communications transcended language in a clear and rich way.

At home, we spoke English almost exclusively, though my parents spoke Spanish amongst themselves, particularly when they wanted to hold a private conversation. In our minds, Spanish was a secret language and I think we felt deprived, left out of an inner circle. Though our parents taught us phrases and occasional words here and there, they abided by their purposeful decision to neither teach nor encourage us to speak Spanish, especially once we started school. Many years later, some time in my mid-20s when I began taking Mexican American Studies courses at the university, I asked them about this rather indignantly. At the time, I was angry at having to, once again, take Spanish in school to recuperate something I felt I should have had as an inheritance if not a birthright. How could they do this to me, I wondered? Didn't they have any idea how embarrassing it was to have to learn Spanish from a gringo, especially when I was surrounded by other whites who somehow seemed to have a better grasp of my "native" tongue than I? Though my siblings and I had raised the question before, it was only when we were adults that they gave us some insight into the painful experiences that shaped their decision. Once we heard their stories, we understood and were able to accept their decision and direct our anger and frustration elsewhere. Born in the late 20s in Houston meant that they had experienced not only the economic hardship of the depression, but the concomitant era of Mexican deportation and accusation of being un-American that everyone, but especially those who were "foreign-looking," faced when they participated in labor strikes or stood in line for government assistance. The Catholic schools they attended in East Houston forbade them to speak Spanish under the threat of corporal punishment or some other form of humiliation. Intimidated, they often suffered in silence. My mom tells the story of how even in high school, despite the fact that she was one of the few graduates in her family, she was so shy about speaking in public that she would ask the teacher to read her work for her rather than suffer the embarrassment of having her accent "corrected" in front of the class.

I cringe now when I think of how 25 years later the nuns at Resurrection Elementary practiced the same pedagogy on their children. I recall some of my classmates being forced to stand in front of class every afternoon and practice saying "chair," "church," "chicken," "children," "shutters," "shine your shoes," and so on so they could improve their enunciation of English and eradicate their Spanish accent. Even now I can vividly picture Sonia Palacios biting her lip trying not to cry as she went through this daily exercise in humiliation. At first some of us thought it was funny, but soon we all became embarrassed of the cruelty of the act. Even as passive witnesses, perhaps because of it, I think we felt partly responsible for her humiliation. Worse yet was when someone would speak Spanish and be punished by having a clothespin put on their lips for five minutes, the same punishment you received if you uttered a profanity. The philosophical and attitudinal shifts resulting from the Bilingual Education Act had yet to take root in our neighborhood. Though years later, I was angry for not knowing Spanish, our ignorance of it as children probably saved us from these indignities. Our parents' decision was strategic, designed as it was to spare us from those humiliations. It did.

Of course the irony in all of this is that our parents could not protect us from the racial hostility we experienced based on the color of our skin and our last name. These made us visible targets for unwanted attention and gave rise to a whole host of conflicted feelings about ourselves, our culture, and our place in the world. Don't get me wrong here. Our parents were not ashamed of being mexicano, nor did they teach us to be. Their social, political, and cultural outlook were formulated in a period now characterized as the Mexican American generation. They believed in self-advocacy and self-reliance. They believed they could simultaneously be proud of their Mexican heritage and be good U.S. citizens. In this way they negotiated the terms of their daily existence as they sought to improve the quality of their lives and create opportunities for their children that they never had. Our culture, as everyone's, was integrated into our daily lives in our religion, music, food, extended familial relations, the way we were taught to honor the living and the dead, and many other customs we practiced. And this culture was integrated within, not apart from, baseball, hotdogs, rock n' roll, the fascination with the exploration of space, in a time when the world around us was changing rapidly in the context of the civil rights movement, the women's movement and the assassination of brave leaders of change.

I think they viewed English language facility, like formal education, as a vehicle of social and economic empowerment. They knew too well from first-hand experience the difficulty and shame that came with trying to unlearn a language and could not see how to create or negotiate an alternative. But our immediate world, defined as it was by the residents of our barrio, was inundated with Spanish in a number of other ways.

As the sixth born child of a family of 8 children (six girls and two boys) education was always stressed by my parents. I grew up a reasonably happy and extrovert boy who had no problem asserting myself and getting my needs met in the world, despite the fact that my parents had lots to worry about and often too little energy, time, and emotional and material resources to share with us. In the 1960s and 1970s, the neighborhood parks were focal points for recreation. It was here in the summers that we participated in summer programs like "Operation Glo" and "Operation PAL," programs that developed our minds and bodies through reading clubs and sports activities. The little Spanish I knew as an adolescent was more appropriate for street talk, Tex-Mex slang, cuss words, vernacular expressions that expressed our in-group solidarity when needed and which we thought were cool. By and large my youthful world was defined by the boundaries of my neighborhood.

Denver Harbor, had experienced white flight, but still had many poor white families and elders who were unable to take advantage of suburbanization programs. I still recall a bully, a white boy a few years older and much taller than me pushing me around as I walked home from church one day when I was about nine. He knocked me down and kept kicking me, laughing and taunting me, calling me "meskin." I eventually got up and ran home, too ashamed to tell my parents what had happened. Despite experiences like this, by and large, this world was ours. Most of us had Anglo friends in the neighborhood with whom we were really close. Bordered by African American neighborhoods, our distinct worlds commingled in limited ways at the park and school.

In East Texas, perhaps in any part but South Texas where Mexicans have long been a majority and proximity to the border means that whites know it's in their economic and political interests to let Spanish and English, Anglos and Mexicans, co-exist, if not in harmony, at least in an uneasy truce, whites turned the word Mexican into a dirty word. The purposeful and snide distortion of Mexican into "meskin" was ubiquitous, circulated as it was in movies like John Wayne's *Alamo*. We were the enemy, the inferior, the inarticulate or mute and insignificant others. Though I didn't appreciate it at the time, I think back now of the creative ways in which this linguistic distortion of our identity was deflected. Foremost in my mind is Larry Juarez's re-appropriation of this word in public places outside of Denver Harbor where we were a visible minority. Be it in a store, at the Astrodome, or in school, or elsewhere, Larry had a way, embarrassing as it was, of anticipating and taking away the force of this perversion of our identity. In these situations he would talk loud, use more Spanish than normal, which always made whites nervous, as if we were plotting against them. Most of all he used to like to call out to us, his friends, in an extraordinarily loud voice, "Hey meskin, what you want to do now?" or "Hey meskin, what you want to eat?" It was his way of preempting the sting when it came from them and proclaiming, "yeah we're here" on our own terms. But those terms weren't always under our control.

One Sunday, walking my girlfriend home along the sidewalk after church, an elderly woman began spraying me with water saying, "Get away, get away from my sidewalk, boy." Shocked, I just stayed there, staring at her as Cindy ran out of the way. When I got home I was soaking wet and this indignity I could not hide from my parents. I was forced to tell them the truth. My father made me go with him over there where he threatened to call the police if they dared to do it again. Though they threatened to spray him too, his refusal to tolerate this was an important lesson in self-defense and righteous indignation.

After attending public middle school, I went to a fairly exclusive all boys Catholic college preparatory school, St. Thomas, which was on the other side of town, far from our barrio and bordering River Oaks, one of the most exclusive neighborhoods in Houston. Life got more complicated there.

Operated by the Basilian fathers, St. Thomas' motto was "Teach me goodness, discipline, and knowledge." I learned, or should I say earned, a lot of discipline and knowledge, but not a lot of goodness. A school comprised of what seemed to be more than 95 percent wealthy whites at the time, I and the few other boys of color, experienced a lot of hostility and were subjected to lots of humiliation due to racism. Most of the time we suffered in silence. Every once in a while the violence erupted into a physical confrontation, but most of the time we faced psychological, emotional and spiritual warfare. And most often we faced it alone. To be sure there were times when we projected onto each other rather than face the force of the majority group's wrath and power.

I'll never forget the first day of high school when Román Pérez and I were standing next to one another in gym and two guys on each side of us kept pushing us into one another. Scared, not knowing how to speak out or disrupt what was happening, we turned to what was familiar, each other, and started fighting. It was just what these guys wanted—for the two "meskins" to make a spectacle of one another. I'm sorry, Román. We had no language to express what was happening to us. We had no social power to leverage our place in this exclusive school; most of us were there on some form of scholarship. So we internalized this and many other indignities. High school turned me into an introvert. I experienced a profound sense of loss of identity and alienation because I came to despise myself. I became ashamed of my parents, my community, my heritage. I lost my voice.

One day in sophomore year of high school, as we were returning from an off-campus excursion, one of my classmates, a would be bully by the name of Rocky Mountain, kept pushing me from behind and hurling the word over and over, "meskin" intended as an insult. Afraid of standing up to him because of the school's zero tolerance policy for fights, and cognizant of how angry and humiliated my parents would be if I was expelled, I took his taunts all the way back to the classroom where we received instructions for the next class and were dismissed. As we left the classroom he did it again and without thinking I turned around and, to everyone's shock, including my own, I punched him in the mouth. He immediately started to bleed and looked to the teacher for help. Our teacher, who I suspect had seen and heard his tauntings, just nodded at us as if to say, go on. Needless to say, we did. But this incident of self-defense did little to alleviate the day to day internalization of cultural self-hate.

Despite many incidents of racial hostility, I also had several very good Anglo friends. I did okay at school and graduated well enough to receive scholarships, but in an unexpressed protest against my family, against the educational system, against myself, I guess, I refused to go to college. If St. Thomas was supposed to be preparing me for college, why would I want to go? Instead I decided to work in a construction equipment rental store, which I excelled at and soon became manager of a newly opened location. It wasn't until several years later that I began taking community college classes part-time. It was then that I remembered how much I liked to read and learn. It took me almost 7 years going to school part-time and working 50 plus hours a week to get my B.A., perhaps because I was a part-time student, but also because I couldn't decide on a major. Finally, when I was 25, my life was profoundly impacted by the first Chicano literature class I ever took. Here, for the first time in 1985, did I realize "we" had a literature and began to contextualize and connect our struggle for survival and cultural preservation.

My ultimate decision to study English and Mexican American Studies was guided by imagination and passion. Reading literature had always offered me a way to broaden my basis of experience, to free myself from constraints and limitations of the real world and to understand that the world was much bigger than my family, and neighborhood. In short, it both broadened my horizons and served as a form of escapism. But in Chicano literature I saw ways to understand the grandeur and the human struggle for existence that made my life, our lives, equally important, equally provocative and rich with philosophy, metaphysical quests for meaning, as well as love, pain, and desire. Mexican American studies and the faculty in those classes showed me that education could be personally and socially empowering. It helped me develop as a human being who felt he had something to say and something meaningful to offer to others. My Chicana/o professors treated me like I was important, like *my* life story and *my* dreams and ideas were worth listening to. I began to feel less insignificant and more responsible for making a difference. Critical thinking, literature, and writing gave shape to my emerging cultural, social, and political awareness. An early credo I learned was the idea that "The more you know, the more you owe." This emerging sense of social responsibility that goes hand in hand with knowledge made me even more thirsty to find a way to make a difference.

Since then, my own process of learning and growing has been ongoing and in many respects completely unforeseen by me—yet as anyone knows who has had to unlearn oppression and negative discourses about oneself, to rediscover oneself, not only is the past always in the present, so is the future. When I completed my B.A. in the winter of 1987, I had no clear idea where I was going. Graduate school was but another way to defer getting a job for a while.

When I headed out to Austin to attend graduate school, all I knew was that I carried within me a love for Chicano literature that had began to help me understand my life in relationship to others. In many respects my pursuit of a graduate degree was a continuation of my effort to discover my self and to find not a profession, but an authentic and meaningful voice for myself that would allow me to not only self-advocate but to contribute to building a better world.

I realize now that many of those public programs I benefited from as a youth were part of the War on Poverty. That was a good war. That was a necessary war, one that still needs to be fought aggressively. As a second generation Mexican American whose grandparents migrated to avoid the ravages of war in Mexico, I am the product of an ongoing war. As peace activists tried to point out then, and need to point out now, the weapons of mass destruction we faced were to be found here at home in under-developed neighborhoods, under-funded schools, the lack of affordable health care for people of all ages, and the list goes on. Born in 1960, my entire life has been marked by U.S. led wars and interventions.

In and out of the classroom experiences have taught me that knowledge is only useful when it can be used in real world situations, to help us understand ourselves or others—and not just understand but to act and to right wrongs if that's what it comes down to. Now, more than ever, I know that knowledge demands responsibility. My parents practiced compadrazgo, the cultural practice of treating friends like extended family that requires working collectively for the greater good. This cultural concept that is my inheritance also undergirds the compromiso we have to speak out, in whatever language, against injustice, including those which compromise language rights.

What I have tried to convey here are experiences which, over time, I have come to realize actually bind me to others, not separate me. These experiences inform and animate my work and empower me to act in the public sphere, not alone but collectively.

My motivation was borne of a series of epiphanies that came with understanding that the real and metaphoric significance of language limitations placed on us are as tangible as the train tracks and freeways that bordered my barrio. These epiphanies led to the realization that certain patterns of legal, structural, social, and economic domination had shaped but not pre-determined my life, and that awareness of them was the first step to dismantling them. Knowledge is power. Knowledge demands responsibility.

In our current historical moment, I cannot help but feel that we live in a time of crisis in which the tolerance level for linguistic, cultural and political diversity is extremely low. As we witness the backlash against free speech that has accompanied the U.S. war against Iraq, the new wave of anti-immigrant hysteria that followed 911, the continued attacks against affirmative action, labor unions, and the stripping of social programs and medical benefits of the elderly, *my conscience tells me we cannot be passive in the face of these actions*. How can we allow the ravaging of peoples rights and say that they don't directly affect us and that these are not our battles? We are called upon to act and to speak out *in whatever language in which people will listen.*

CONTRIBUTOR BIOS

Carlos C. Amaya teaches Spanish at the Foreign Languages Department at Eastern Illinois University. He was born in El Salvador but immigrated to the United States at the end of the 1980's when the devastating civil war was claiming the lives of young people. He studied at the Catholic University (UCA) "José Simeón Cañas" that was targeted by the army in 1989 for its criticism of the human right abuses by the government. His works have been included in *Chiricu*, a journal published by Chicano-Riqueño Studies at Indiana University, and *Revista del Ateneo* in Puerto Rico.

Rane Arroyo is a Gay Puerto Rican poet, the author of five books of poetry, including *Home Movies of Narcissus* (University of Arizona Press). His newest book, *The Portable Famine* won the 2004 John Ciardi Poetry Prize and has been published by BkMk Press. A book of gay short stories, *How To Name A Hurricane,* is also out on University of Arizona Press. He writes in Toledo, Ohio where he is working on his memoirs and poems about Roswell, New Mexico.

Aureliano De Soto was born and raised in Highland Park, Los Angeles, where he attended the city's public schools. He received his BA from Yale in 1990, and went on to do his graduate work at the History of Consciousness program at the University of California, Santa Cruz. He currently teaches at Metropolitan State University in St. Paul, Minnesota.

Lorena Duarte was born in El Salvador and immigrated as a child to Minnesota with her family. She holds a degree in Hispanic Studies/Romance Languages and Literature from Harvard University and now lives in Minneapolis where she is the former editor of *La Prensa de Minnesota*, a bilingual Latino newspaper. Aside from poetry, she is active in several organizations that focus on the issues of community and social justice.

Margarita Engle is a botanist and a Cuban-American author of three novels, *The Poet Slave of Cuba* (Henry Holt & Co.), *Singing to Cuba* (Arté Público Press) and *Skywriting* (Bantam). Her work is published in a variety of anthologies, and in journals such as *Atlanta Review, Bilingual Review, Blue Mesa Review*, and *California Quarterly* among others. Engle lives with her family in central California.

Olga A. García Echeverría was born and raised in East Los Angeles, California. She has a BA in Ethnic Studies and an MFA in Creative Writing. During the past ten years, she has had the opportunity to read her work throughout California, in Texas, Mexico City, New York, North Carolina, Minnesota, and France. Her poetry appears on two Calaca Press CD's *Raza Spoken Here: poesía chicana volume 1* and *When Skin Peels*. Her book, *Falling Angels: Cuentos y Poemas*, is forthcoming.

Rudy H. Garcia is a life-long resident of the South Texas town of Port Isabel. An educator for the past twenty years, he has a B.S. in psychology from Pan American University (U.T. Pan American) and a Masters in Guidance and Counseling from the University of Texas at Brownsville. He is a member of the Narciso Martinez Cultural Arts Center writers' forum in San Benito, Texas.

Vida Mia García received her BA in English and Women's Studies from Brown University, and is currently ABD in the Program in Modern Thought and Literature at Stanford University. One of the most important pieces of writing she has ever come across is the author's bio in *The House on Mango Street*; the final sentence effectively set her life's course.

Nuvia Crisol Guerra has worked as a molecular biologist research associate for a San Diego pharmaceutical company ever since she received her degree in Biochemistry/Cell Biology from UCSD in 2000. Her artistic work has been featured in numerous galleries, murals, posters, and magazine covers. Born in Paramount, California, Crisol makes her home in San Diego. Most recently, Crisol has been promoting her game Loteria de Mujer.

Celeste Guzman Mendoza is a native of San Antonio, Texas. Her poetry has appeared in the following publications: *¡Floricanto si!: An Anthology of Latina Poetry*; *Cande, te estoy llamando*; and *Red Boots and Attitude: An Anthology of Texas Female Writers*. She graduated from Barnard College with a double major in English Literature and Theatre. She will graduate in January 2007 with a MFA degree in poerty from the Bennington Writing Seminars.

Leticia Hernández-Linares was born in Los Angeles and now lives and writes in San Francisco. Her writing has appeared in anthologies and literary journals such as *This Bridge We Call Home, Latino Literature Today, Crab Orchard Review,* and *Puerto del Sol. Razor Edges of my Tongue,* her chapbook of poetry, is available from Calaca Press. She has performed at universities and community art venues throughout the country and in El Salvador. A Ph.d. candidate in Literature at the University of Pennsylvania, she has worked as an educator and youth advocate for over fifteen years. She is currently the Executive Director of Making Waves in Marin County.

Ana M. Lara is an AfroDominican American writer and organizer. She was born in the Dominican Republic, raised in East Africa and Mount Vernon, NY. She received her BA from Harvard University. Ana's critical writing has appeared in several anthologies and journals and she is the co-author of bustingbinaries.com: a website addressing binary thinking in U.S. based social justice movements. Her debut novel, *Erzulie's Skirt* (Redbone Press), was published in October 2006. Her website is www.zorashorse.com. She lives in Austin, TX.

Luis Larios Vendrell nació en Madrid. En 1965 consiguió un puesto de "Lector" en Irlanda y más tarde se trasladó a Escocia. Desde 1968 reside en los Estados Unidos donde ha enseñado español en diversas universidades e institutos. Aún después de tan larga residencia en países de habla inglesa, su obra literaria es exclusivamente en castellano.

Stephanie Li is an assistant professor of English at the University of Rochester where she teaches American literature and creative writing. After teaching high school English for two years in California, she received her M.F.A. and Ph.D. from Cornell University. Her M.F.A. thesis, *Ombligo,* examines issues of family and identity resulting from the narrator's mixed cultural heritage. Stephanie's academic research interests include representations of race and gender, forms of individual and collective resistance, and narratives of immigration and assimilation.

Paul Martínez Pompa received his B.A. from the University of

Chicago and his M.F.A. from Indiana University. He currently teaches English and creative writing at Triton College in River Grove, Illinois. In 2006 Momotombo Press released Martínez Pompa's poetry chapbook, Pepper Spray. He resides on the northwest side of Chicago.

Melani "Mele" Martinez, born in Tucson, Arizona, holds an M.F.A. in Creative Nonfiction from Goucher College in Baltimore, Maryland. She recently received Fourth Genre's Annual Editor's Prize for her essay, "The Molino." She was an original member of Yjastros: The American Flamenco Repertory Co. and currently teaches flamenco in Tucson, Arizona.

Cecilia Méndez is an artist and educator from Massachusetts. She has worked as an art educator at the Centro Educativo Ix-tliyollotl in Puebla, Mexico; at the Addison Gallery of American Art in Anodver Massachusetts; and at the University of Michigan School of Art & Design in partnership with Detroit Public Schools. She received a BA with Honors in Visual Art from Brown University in 1996 and an MFA from the University of Michigan in 2002. She is currently the Director of Exhibitions at the New Art Center in Newton, MA.

Louis G. Mendoza, originally from Houston, TX, is Associate Professor and chair of the Department of Chicano Studies at the University of Minnesota. His areas of expertise are Chicana/o Literature, Cultural Studies, and Prison Literatures. In addition to numerous articles and reviews, he has published three books, *Historia: The Literary Making of Chicana and Chicano History, Crossing into America: The New Literature of Immigration* (co-edited with S. Shankar), *Raúlsalinas and the Jail Machine: Selected Writings (1959-1974)*.

Orlando Ricardo Menes teaches in the Creative Writing Program at the University of Notre Dame. New poems have appeared in *Prairie Schooner*, *Epoch*, *North American Review*, and *River Styx*. Recent books are a poetry collection, *Furia* (Milkweed, 2005), and the edited anthology *Renaming Ecstasy: Latino Writings on the Sacred* (Bilingual Press/Editorial Bilingüe, 2004).

Oscar Mireles has published over 100 poems and a chapbook of poems titled Second Generation (Focus Communications, 1985).

He is the editor of two anthologies titled *I didn't know there were Latinos in Wisconsin: 20 Hispanic poets in 1989* and *I didn't know there were Latinos in Wisconsin: 30 Hispanic writers* in 1999. He is a member of the Minds Eye Poetry Group that produces a monthly poetry radio show on community radio station WORT.

Rosie Molinary earned her MFA from Goddard College. She lives in Davidson, NC where she is a freelance writer and teaches creative writing. Her book *Hijas Americanas: Beauty, Body, Image & Growing Up* will be republished by Seal Press in May 2007.

Teresa Nasarre nace en una pequeña ciudad medieval en España. Entusiasta del poder de la palabra para ponernos en contacto con nuestros deseos, los de nuestra comunidad y el resto del mundo, escribe y realiza talleres literarios en Nueva York donde vive actualmente. Muy joven consiguió el premio literario cazuelas del arte (Universidad Zaragoza 1987) y desde entonces colabora en periódicos y revistas. Su primera novela *Al otro lado* acreedora del premio a la creatividad en España (2000) tambien ha ganado el 6th Latin Book Awards (Chicago, 2004) a la mejor novela de misterio publicada en español el año anterior.

Toni Nelson Herrera studies history and other subjects that interest her. She has academic connections to both UT-Austin and the University of Minnesota, Twin Cities, but more importantly she feels connected to the natural beauty, environmental preservation, and great spaces each city provides for opportunities for wonderful outdoor athletic fun. She is saving up money to take yet another Summer Language program.

Roberto Pachecano enrolled at St. Mary's University to work on a degree in English Communication Arts after a career with the US Postal Service was cut short in 1999 due to a relapse of an old service-connected disability. He graduated Cum Laude May 10, 2003, thirty-three years after his first attempt at a formal education. His essays, poems, and short stories have been published in *amarillobay*, *Distant Echoes*, *Pecan Grove Review*, *San Antonio Express-News*, *Texas Hispanic Journal*, and *Texas Vietnam Veterans Magazine*.

Elizabeth Pérez is a doctoral candidate at the University of Chicago Divinity School, focusing on religious formations of the

African Diaspora. Her dissertation will examine the intersection of ethnomedical healing, female leadership, and conversion in Afro-Cuban Santería. She has published poetry in the *Bilingual Review/Revista Bilingüe*, the award-winning anthology *El Coro: A Chorus of Latino/a Poetry* (edited by Martín Espada, 1997), and elsewhere.

Maria Elena Perez was born to a Dominican mother and a Puerto Rican father in Brooklyn, New York. She obtained her M.S.W. from the Hunter College School of Social Work and currently works full-time at a community based organization in New York City that responds to the needs of immigrants through direct services and direct action. Maria Elena loves to dance and dream. She still calls Brooklyn home.

Margarita E. Pignataro is a Florida State University Alumni. She is working towards a Ph.D. at Arizona State University in Chicano Literature/Theatre with a minor in Religious Studies. She is of Chilean, Bolivian, Aymara and Italian descent and has relatives from Caribbean and other South American countries.

If she ever becomes fluent in Spanish, **Beth Rodriguez** will then tackle Swedish and Italian, so she can speak to all branches of her family. She graduated from Smith College in 2002, majoring in Women's Studies and minoring in Spanish.

Joe Sainz is a full-time college faculty in the area of business computer applications. Besides writing, designing and self-publishing *A Personal Checklist for Life* (a humor book), he has also written numerous non-fiction pieces, including a short piece in the *Don't Sweat the Small Stuff* series and a winning entry in *Writer's Digest's Your Assignment*, among others. He has also written short stories, poetry, educational articles and two 80,000-word novels.

raúlrsalinas is a prominent literary voice who has also been a tireless crusader for human rights and social justice. Author of four poetry collections and three spoken words CD's. His literary work has appeared in numerous anthologies and journals. His most recent publications are: *raúlrsalinas and the Jail Machine: My Weapon is My Pen, selected writings by Raul Salinas*, edited by Louis G. Mendoza (UT-Press) and Indio Trails: A Xicano Odyssey through Indian Country (Wings Press). An award winning writer, he has received numerous acknowledgements, including the NALAC (National Association of Latino Art and Culture) lifetime achievement award. Currently he is an adjunct professor at St. Edwards University in Austin, Texas.

Edwin Torres, from New York City, is a recipient of fellowships from The New York Foundation for the Arts and The Foundation for Contemporary Performance Art. He's taught workshops at Naropa Institute and The St. Marks Poetry Project and has published in many journals and anthologies. Author of *The All-Union Day of the Shock Worker* (Roof Books) among other titles, his CDs include *Holy Kid* (Kill Rock Stars) and *NOVO* (www.oozebap.org). Edwin is co-editor of the journal *Rattapallax*.

Liliana Valenzuela, born and raised in Mexico City, is an adopted tejana. She translated *Caramelo* by Sandra Cisneros, is the recipient of the Christina Sergeyevna Award for best poem, and the Chicano/Latino Literary Prize for best short story. She has three poetry chapbooks or "libritos" entitled *Bocas palabras* (winner of the Voces Selectas award), *Mujer frontera, mujer Malinche*, and *The Poetry of Rice Fields*. She lives in Austin, Texas, with her family.

Steve Werkmeister, the matrilineal grandson of Mexican immigrants and patrilineal great-grandson of German immigrants, was born and raised in Nebraska. Werkmeister received his M.A. from the University of Nebraska-Lincoln and is completing work on a PhD, also at UNL. A published poet, Werkmeister is currently an Assistant Professor at Johnson County Community College in Overland Park, Kansas. He lives in Olathe, Kansas with his family.